Karl Friedrich Schinkel
Ludwig Persius
Friedrich August Stüler

Karl Friedrich Schinkel
Ludwig Persius
Friedrich August Stüler

Bauten in Berlin und Potsdam
Buildings in Berlin and Potsdam

Photographien
Photographs
Hillert Ibbeken

Einführung
Introduction
Barry Bergdoll

Edition Axel Menges

© 2013 Edition Axel Menges, Stuttgart/London
ISBN 978-3-936681-72-7

Reproduktionen/Reproductions: Gabór Mocsonoky,
Budapest (Schinkel); Kleiber Studio, Fellbach (Persius);
L & N Litho, Waiblingen (Stüler)
Druck und Bindearbeiten/Printing and binding:
Graspo CZ, a.s., Zlín, Tschechische Republik/Czech
Republic

Übersetzung ins Englische/Translation into English:
Michael Robinson, Ilze Klavina
Übersetzung des Essays von Barry Bergdoll ins Deut-
sche/Translation of the essay by Barry Bergdoll into
German: Hillert Ibbeken
Lektorat/Editorial work: Dorothea Duwe
Gestaltung/Design: Axel Menges

Vorwort

Das hier vorgelegte Buch ist eine Synopse, eine Zusammenfassung der ebenfalls in der Edition Axel Menges erschienenen Bücher über die preußischen Architekten Karl Friedrich Schinkel (1781–1841), Ludwig Persius (1803–1845) und Friedrich August Stüler (1800–1865), beschränkt sich aber auf die Berliner und Potsdamer Werke dieser Architekten. Die drei genannten Bücher haben den Untertitel »Das architektonische Werk heute«, es geht dort also ausschließlich um noch existierende Bauten. Das gilt auch für die vorliegende Auswahl. Die Frage, ob diese Auswahl und Beschränkung auf Berlin und Potsdam auch repräsentativ für das Werk der drei Architekten ist, kann klar mit einem Ja beantwortet werden. Für Persius stellt sich diese Frage gar nicht erst, weil er in seinem kurzen Leben fast ausschließlich in Potsdam und dessen unmittelbarer Umgebung gebaut hat. Stülers Werk reicht von Köln am Rhein bis in die Masuren, dazu kommen bedeutende Gebäude in Stockholm und Budapest. Rund ein Viertel seiner Werke steht in Potsdam und Berlin. Das wahrhaft gigantische Lebenswerk von Schinkel reicht von Aachen bis St. Petersburg. Berlin und Potsdam besitzen rund ein Drittel seiner Werke. Man kann aber getrost sagen, wer den Schinkel, den Persius und den Stüler in Berlin und Potsdam kennt, jeweils auch den ganzen Architekten kennt. Da die hier versammelten Bilder in den sieben Jahren von 1998 bis 2005 aufgenommen wurden, sind sie selber schon ein wenig historisch geworden.

Hillert Ibbeken

Foreword

This book is a synopsis, a summary of the books also published by Edition Axel Menges about the Prussian architects Karl Friedrich Schinkel (1781 to 1841), Ludwig Persius (1803–1845) and Friedrich August Stüler (1800–1865), but it covers only the works of these architects in Berlin and Potsdam. The three books mentioned above are subtitled »The architectural work today«; in other words, they are exclusively about buildings that still exist. This is also true of the present selection. The question whether this selection and limitation to Berlin and Potsdam is representative of the work of the three architects can clearly be answered in the affirmative. For Persius this question does not even arise, because during his short life he has built almost exclusively in Potsdam and its immediate vicinity. Stüler's work is found in a region extending from Cologne on the Rhine to Masuria, with some important buildings in Stockholm and Budapest as well. About a quarter of his works can be found in Potsdam and Berlin. The truly gigantic lifework of Schinkel extends from Aachen to St. Petersburg. Berlin and Potsdam have about a third of his works. It can be confidently said, however, that those who know the works of Schinkel, Persius and Stüler in Berlin and Potsdam also know the architect's work as a whole in each case. Since the pictures assembled here were taken between 1998 and 2005, they themselves have already become somewhat historical.

Hillert Ibbeken

Barry Bergdoll

»... das letzte große, allumfassende Genie, das die Architektur hervorbrachte.« Karl Friedrich Schinkel und seine Schüler im Angesicht der modernen Bewegung

Nur wenige Entwicklungen der Architektur des 19. Jahrhunderts provozierten unterschiedlichere Auffassungen in der Architekturrezeption als die der Berliner Schule von Schinkel und seinen unmittelbaren Nachfolgern, unter denen der frühverstorbene Ludwig Persius und der überaus produktive Friedrich August Stüler eine herausragende Position einnehmen. Nun, da das Werk dieses Trios, das in der Berliner Architektur für mehr als ein halbes Jahrhundert den Ton angab, durch die Erkundungen von Hillert Ibbeken zusammengestellt wurde, steht vor uns das Schwarzweißbild einer jahrzehntelangen stilistischen Tradition, die um die Mitte des 19. Jahrhunderts internationale Aufmerksamkeit auf Berlin lenkte, jener Stadt, die dank ihrer spezifischen Baukultur mit Paris, dessen Beaux-Arts-Tradition ebenfalls Einfluß auf das internationale Baugeschehen ausübte, durchaus rivalisieren konnte. Wurde im frühen 20. Jahrhundert das Erbe der École des Beaux-Arts jedoch als akademisch angegriffen – ebenso wie die englische Neogotik wegen ihres Historismus –, blieb das Vermächtnis von Schinkel und seinen Nachfolgern von dieser allgemeinen Ablehnung der Baukultur des 19. Jahrhunderts meist ausgenommen. Für Hermann Muthesius, der in seiner Stilarchitektur und Baukunst 1902 die Übel des Eklektizismus diagnostizierte, der vieles von der Architektur des 19. Jahrhunderts bedrohe, war Schinkel »das letzte umfassende Genie, das die Architektur hervorgebracht hatte, sozusagen der letzte Großarchitekt« (Muthesius 1902, S. 15), ein klarer Ausgangspunkt für die Reform moderner Baupraxis. Muthesius betrachtete die Stadt Berlin als die große Ausnahme in der Entwicklung der Architektur des 19. Jahrhunderts, wobei die Schinkelschule ein wahres Bollwerk gegen stilistischen Eklektizismus und Oberflächlichkeit bilde.

Diese Sichtweise stellte im Vergleich zur Rezeption der Werke, wie sie noch zu Lebzeiten der Architekten vorherrschend gewesen war, eine radikale Umkehr dar. Denn in der Mitte des 19. Jahrhunderts erfreuten sich sowohl die klassizistischen öffentlichen Gebäude von Schinkel und Stüler als auch der von Schinkel und Persius perfektionierte asymmetrische Villentyp internationalen Einflusses als hochentwickelte Modelle der Übernahme historischer Stile für moderne Nutzungen. Besonders in der Mode der asymmetrischen italienischen Villa um die Jahrhundertmitte war der Einfluß der Berliner Schule weithin zu erkennen. Schinkel genoß internationale Anerkennung durch die Kupferstiche seiner Sammlung Architektonischer Entwürfe, die ihren Weg weit in den Norden, bis nach Schottland fand. Hier ließ sich Alexander »der Grieche« Thomson nicht nur von Schinkels strenger, rasterähnlicher Durchfensterung einiger seiner Kirchen und kommerziellen Gebäude inspirieren, sondern auch von der pittoresken Massierung des Hofgärtnerhauses von Schinkel und Persius bei seiner meisterhaften Villa Holmwood in Glasgow, 1857/58, die kürzlich restauriert wurde. Einige Jahre später vermachte Thomson seine Ausgabe von Schinkels großer Mappe der Glasgow Architectural Society. Während jedoch Schinkels Einfluß in den Details vieler strenger Zeichnungen von Thomson im modernen neogriechischen Stil, besonders in Holmwood, offensichtlich ist, verschmolz er ihn

gründlich mit der althergebrachten britischen Liebe zur Tradition der pittoresken, italienisierenden Villa – was sich zumindest bis zum Werk von John Nash zu Beginn des Jahrhunderts zurückverfolgen läßt. (Stamp 1938.)

Der Einfluß der Potsdamer Villen von Persius ist bis hin zu den Details unverkennbar in dem oft dem Architekten Ithiel Town zugeschriebenen Haus Alsop (1838 bis 1840) in Wesleyan, Connecticut, zu erkennen, wobei es sich dort um den seltenen Fall einer unverfälschten Einwirkung handelt. Mitte der 1850er Jahre – als der amerikanische Architekt Henry van Brunt einen weitverbreiteten Einfluß deutscher Architektur-Periodika auf die Bauplanung in Amerika feststellte – wurden die Bände jener beiden großen Kompendien, welche die neuen asymmetrischen Kompositionen und die Abkehr von landestypischen Details in Berlin und Potsdam perfektionierten, nämlich das Architektonische Album (1840–62) und besonders das weitverbreitete Architektonische Skizzenbuch (1852–66), in den fortschrittlichen New Yorker Architekturbüros intensiv konsultiert. Exemplare dieser Werke, wie auch der Entwürfe zu Kirchen, Pfarr- und Schulbauten, die die Bauformen amerikanischer protestantischer Kirchen eindeutig mitbestimmt hatten, fanden sich nicht nur in der Astor Library in New York, sondern auch als Standardquellen in einigen der bedeutendsten New Yorker Büros, so bei P. B. Wight, Edward T. Potter und wahrscheinlich auch bei Russel Sturgis. (Landau 1983, S. 273.) Die Tradition des Trios Schinkel / Persius / Stüler war ein nicht wegzudenkender Bestandteil der pittoresken Komposition und zwanglosen Raumgestaltung, die mit der Entstehung der amerikanischen Bäderarchitektur verbunden werden, besonders mit den frühen Villen in Newport von Richard Morris Hunt und seinen Nachfolgern – einer Entwicklung, die lange als wichtiger Ausgangspunkt für die Erprobung neuer Planungs- und Entwurfsmethoden im Frühwerk von Frank Lloyd Wright betrachtet wurde.

Die Wandlung des Schinkel-Vermächtnisses von einer Entwurfsquelle zum kämpferischen Eintreten für die Authentizität des Ausdrucks und die Überwindung der historischen Formensprache wurde in Amerika ebenfalls vorangetrieben, sogar noch bevor sie sich zum wahren Leitmotiv der Reformergeneration der deutschen Moderne um die Wende zum 20. Jahrhundert entwickelte. Vor allem in Chicago, das nicht nur zur Wiege der modernen amerikanischen Architektur wurde, sondern dessen Kultur im 19. Jahrhundert auch eine der am stärksten von Deutschen geprägten in Amerika war, bestimmte Schinkels Erbe die lokale Architekturdiskussion. Nur vier Jahre nach Stülers Tod begann der deutsche Auswanderer Frederick Baumann (1826–1921) von seiner Ankunft in Chicago im Jahr 1850 bis zur Entwicklung der technischen Innovationen für den Hochhausbau (besonders der Einzelgründung, die sich zumindest bis zu Schinkels Altem Museum als preußische Lösung für das Bauen auf sandigem Boden zurückführen läßt) aktiv das Erbe der Schinkelschen Suche nach tektonischer Reinheit als wegweisende Kraft bei der Gestaltung der Architektur der Gegenwart zu pflegen. 1869 veröffentlichte Baumann eine gekürzte Übersetzung der »Schinkelfestrede« von Friedrich Adler aus demselben Jahr. Es war der erste von mehreren Texten, die in den Architekturzeitschriften Chicagos erschienen und Schinkel als einen Vorläufer der Architektur der Moderne priesen, in der Tat als den Vertreter architektonischer Nüchternheit und Sachlichkeit, die den pragmatischen Geist in der Errichtung

von Geschäftshäusern verkörperten, welcher bei der Bebauung von Chicagos Downtown vorherrschen sollte. Adler wies besonders auf den Umstand hin, daß Schinkels Bauakademie frei von historischen Bezügen sei, und bewunderte seine »stilreine Strenge, nüchterne Schönheit ... und fesselnde Originalität«, die es einem »Samen vergleichbar macht, der weiteres organisches Wachstum verspricht.« (Adler 1869, S. 199.) Indem Adler und Baumann das von Muthesius entwickelte Thema um beinahe zwei Jahrzehnte vorwegnahmen, prägten sie die Vorstellung von Schinkel als einem Vorläufer ehrlichen und sachlichen Bauens, der mit den Gegebenheiten des Materials und modernen räumlichen Bedürfnissen umzugehen verstand und wenig Sinn für die Nostalgie der Wiederbelebung historischer Stile hatte.

In Deutschland wurden die ersten Jahre des 20. Jahrhunderts, geprägt von einer intensiven Erneuerung des Interesses an Schinkels Architektur, in erster Linie von dem Glauben geleitet, daß, sobald man die letzten Funken des preußischen Klassizismus entfacht habe, der Weg zu einem wahren kulturellen Ausdruck für das moderne Deutschland geebnet werden könne. Wohl keiner hat Schinkels Bedeutung als Wegweiser zur Abkehr von der historistischen Kultur so klar formuliert wie Adolf Loos, als er 1910 von ihm sagte: »Wir haben ihn vergessen. Möge das Licht dieser überragenden Gestalt auf unsere kommende Baukünstlergeneration fallen.« (Loos 1910, S. 317.) Vielleicht traf dies auf das Wien von Loos zu, aber in der deutschen Hauptstadt war Schinkel zu keiner Zeit vom Thron gestoßen worden, wie der Kritiker Paul Westheim 1913 in einem Leitartikel »Schinkel und die Gegenwart« schrieb. Die Gefahr lag, wie Westheim meinte, nicht darin, daß die Architekten Schinkel vergessen hätten, sondern darin, daß sein Andenken durch Nachahmung verunglimpft würde. »Aber ist es mehr als architektonische Künstelei, was da unter der Marke ›Schinkel‹ in Berlin als dernier cri an die Straßen gestellt wird?«, spottete er. (Westheim 1913, S. B 83.)

1913 stimmte Westheim außerdem in einen Chor von Stimmen ein, die die ideologische Uneinigkeit in den laufenden Debatten zu überdecken suchten. Eine ganze, von Friedrich Nietzsches Angriff auf den Historismus und der anhaltenden Begeisterung für Julius Langbehns Rembrandt als Erzieher (1890) inspirierte Generation blickte auf Schinkel als Teil dessen, was Paul Mebes 1908 als »Architektur und Kunstgewerbe im letzten Jahrhundert ihrer natürlichen Entwicklung« bezeichnete. Sein Buch Um 1800, 1908 erstmals publiziert, aber bis 1925 dreimal wieder aufgelegt, diente als bester Vermittler dafür. Es war Mebes' Ziel, die Aufmerksamkeit auf die anonyme Architektur der vorigen Jahrhundertwende zu lenken: als Anker in dem Verwirrung stiftenden Sturm der laufenden Debatte, um gegenüberzustellen, was er als Krise der Authentizität bei der sich modernisierenden bürgerlichen Kultur zu erkennen glaubte. Ihm genügte es, durch irgendeines der neuen Viertel deutscher Städte zu spazieren, um die volle Wirkung der Krise zu spüren, die sich nicht nur im totalen Verlust architektonischen Ausdrucks äußerte, sondern auch im Verlust einer ganzen Geisteshaltung, die genauso das Vermächtnis einer Kultur darstellt wie ihre Monumente. Für Mebes, wie auch für Muthesius, lag eine der großen Gefahren der Beschleunigung der industriellen Revolution in der Fähigkeit, Stile zu imitieren, ohne die konstruktiven Systeme und die gesellschaftliche Bedeutung zu verstehen, die ihren Formen innewohnen. Die Lösung für die Architekten bestehe darin, die im frühen 19. Jahrhunderts gebrochene Tradition der Architektur zu erneuern. In den meisten Fällen erfolgte dies in Form unprätentiöser, regional gestalteter Bauten, aber Schinkels Name war der einzige, den Mebes in ein Kompendium von mehreren hundert Beispielen für nicht eindeutig unprätentiöses »bürgerliches« Bauen des späten 18. und frühen 19. Jahrhunderts aufnahm. 1918, als Mebes eine zweite, erweiterte Edition herausgab, tat er sich mit Walter Curt Behrendt zusammen, der zu einem der großen Bauhaus-Protagonisten der 1920er Jahre wurde. Behrendt stellte fest, daß das allgemeine Interesse am Neoklassizismus im Begriff sei, zu einer neuen Art von »Internationalem Stil« zu werden, und daß »es etwas in der geistigen Planung geben muß, das die zeitgenössische Architektur mit der Zeit um 1800 so verbindet, daß wir dort einen natürlichen Anfangspunkt finden für die Konfrontation mit den Herausforderungen unserer modernen Welt.« (Mebes 1918.)

Niemand erfüllte diese Forderung vor dem Ersten Weltkrieg besser als Peter Behrens, in dessen Büro in Neubabelsberg Ludwig Mies van der Rohe, Charles Edouard Jeanneret (der spätere Le Corbusier) und Walter Gropius in den Jahren zwischen 1908 und 1912 zeitweilig arbeiteten. Noch bevor Behrens 1907 von Düsseldorf nach Berlin ging, um den berühmten Auftrag anzunehmen, die Gebäude, die Produkte und das Erscheinungsbild der AEG umzugestalten, pries der führende Kunstkritiker Julius Meier-Graefe den von Behrens vertretenen Klassizismus und wünschte, er würde allgemein verbreitet werden, um eine weitergehende Erneuerung der Architektur zu befördern. »Sollte es nicht möglich sein, so zu bauen, daß keinerlei Form, sondern nur der kühle Geist der Griechen dabei entsteht, der Andacht wert?« (Anderson 2001, S. 118.) Fritz Schumacher, der 1901 einen wichtigen Beitrag über Tradition und Innovation geschrieben hatte, erinnerte sich Jahre später an einen Besuch bei Behrens in Neubabelsberg und erwähnte, daß dieser ihn mitgenommen hatte, um »seine geliebten kleinen Schinkel-Gebäude zu zeigen.« (Schumacher 1944, S. 22, zitiert auf englisch von Anderson 2001, S. 116.) Die stärkste Verbundenheit von Behrens mit der Berliner klassizistischen Tradition zeigte sich 1911/12. Es war in der Tat auch der Höhepunkt der Verherrlichung Schinkels in Berliner Architekturkreisen. Zu dieser Zeit errichtete Behrens gleichzeitig zwei größere Gebäude, deren formale und räumliche Qualitäten sich direkt auf Schinkels Ideen bezogen, und zwar in der Suche nach einer architektonischen Sprache innerhalb der Tradition anstelle der Imitation von Bauformen eines ganzen Schinkelgebäudes oder seiner Teile. Sowohl beim Haus Wiegand in Berlin-Dahlem als auch beim Mannesmann-Verwaltungsgebäude in Düsseldorf orientierte sich Behrens an Schinkels Suche nach einem abstrakten und grundlegenden Ordnungssystem, das sich zwar an den Ordnungen ausrichten, aber jeden eindeutigen Klassizismus vermeiden sollte. Beim Haus Wiegand zeigt sich Behrens' intensive Suche nach einer elementaren Ordnung in der einem Schottenmuster ähnelnden Verflechtung von Innen- und Außenräumen, von Haus und Garten, wie sie Schinkel und Persius beim Hofgärtnerhaus von Schloß Charlottenburg in Sanssouci (1829 bis 1833) gelungen war. Schon 1861 pries Stüler Charlottenhof als etwas, »das zum Originellsten gehört, was je im Sinne vergangener Zeit vom Standpunkt der jetzigen Kunst aus erdacht und ausgeführt wurde.« (Stüler 1861, S. 19.) In einer Rezension des Hauses Wiegand, in der einflußreichen Zeitschrift *Innendekoration* er-

schien, sieht der Architekturkritiker Robert Breuer Behrens im Gleichgewicht mit der Vergangenheit und der Zukunft der Architektur und gleichzeitig als einen »Prophet[en] der Form« und den »Erfüller von Schinkel.« (Breuer 1913, zitiert in Anderson 2001, S. 119.) Als sich die Gebäude der Vollendung näherten, erschien die erste Monographie über Schinkel seit dem 19. Jahrhundert im bedeutenden Berliner Verlag Wasmuth, gezeichnet mit Fritz Stahl, dem gerade angenommenen Pseudonym des Kritikers Siegfried Lilienthal. »Diese Schrift ist aus der Überzeugung entstanden, daß Carl Friedrich Schinkel der ›kommende Mann‹ unserer Baukunst ist, und daß es für den Architekten keine dringendere Angelegenheit gibt, als ihn und seine Werke recht zu kennen. Ruhm und Einfluß, die er im Leben und noch fünfzig Jahre nach seinem Tode gehabt hat, so groß sie waren, sind nichts im Vergleich zu dem Ruhm und dem Einfluß, die er noch haben wird. Wie alle Genies war er der Menschheit um ein Jahrhundert voraus. Die mit und unmittelbar nach ihm lebten, konnten sich nur ein Teil von ihm wirklich aneignen. Bis wir sein ganzes Wesen von seinem Kern aus begreifen konnten, mußten wir durch viele Schulen gehen. Wer weiß, wie spät die Deutschen goethereif geworden sind, wird sich nicht darüber wundern, daß erst wir schinkelreif geworden sein sollen.« (Stahl 1911, S. 3.) 1927 lobte Behrens bei der jährlichen Schinkelfestrede mit dem Titel »Zum Problem der technischen und tektonischen Beziehungen« Le Corbusier und sagte abschließend: »Hierin spricht ein moderner Geist, der sich selbst dem Idealismus anvertraut, und hierbei sind wir zu dem Mann zurückgekehrt, der Schönheit suchte und Sachlichkeit stiftete, zu Carl Friedrich Schinkel.« (Posener 1981, S. 290.)

Obwohl Mies diesem Programm auch in seinen Vorkriegsgebäuden wie dem Haus Perls in Zehlendorf von 1911, das eindeutig auf den Schinkelpavillon in Charlottenburg zurückgeht, unmittelbar folgte, bewegte er sich dennoch unmerklich im Strom der von Paul Westheim 1913 ausgelösten Schinkel-Renaissance, wobei dieser die Architekten aufgefordert hatte, mehr in das Wesen des Schinkelschen Formempfindens einzudringen, anstatt die äußeren Merkmale seines Baustils zu übernehmen. Vierzehn Jahre später griff Westheim in einem Mies van der Rohe gewidmeten Artikel, der ersten jemals publizierten Untersuchung über die Bauten der sich formierenden Architektur-Avantgarde, das Thema von Schinkels anhaltendem Einfluß in der inzwischen stark veränderten Berliner Architekturszene wieder auf. Auch wenn Mies damals, 1927, sowohl sich als auch seinen Stil radikal umgeformt hatte – er schloß gerade seine Aufgabe als Direktor der Ausstellung in der Weißenhofsiedlung in Stuttgart ab –, kam Westheim auf Mies' Ankunft 1905 in Berlin zurück – das Berlin der Schinkel-Renaissance – und argumentierte, daß, obwohl »Mies von einem Schinkelstil gar nichts mehr hat«, er aber dennoch »einer der begabtesten weil ursprünglichsten Schinkelschüler« (Westheim 1927, S. 57) sei, eben weil er erfülle, was er, Westheim, schon 1913 gefordert hatte: keine Nachahmung von Schinkels Formenrepertoire, sondern eher eine Verpflichtung für Schinkels »erstaunliches Gefühl für Masse, Verhältnisse, Rhythmen und Formenwohllaut.« (Westheim 1927, S. 53.) 1927 stellte Westheim in dieser Analyse fest: »Mies, der sich Schinkel nähert und ihn zunächst wie üblich auffaßt als Mittler einer bestimmten Formensprache, entdeckt für sich hinter diesem klassizistischen Schinkel jenen anderen Schinkel, der im Sinne und mit den technischen und handwerklichen Mit-

teln seiner Zeit ein eminent sachlicher Baumeister gewesen ist. ... Das ist es, was das Alte Museum von Schinkel zu einem so ausgezeichneten Museumsbau gemacht hat, und was die Nationalgalerie als Bau eines sogenannten Schinkel-Schülers, dem der Stil und nicht die Sache das Entscheidende war, zu einem so unrettbar verpfuschten Museumsbau macht.« (Westheim 1927, S. 56.)

Als Muthesius in seiner *Stilarchitektur* Schinkel als »das letzte, umfassende Genie, das die Architektur hervorbrachte«, bezeichnete, fügte er noch schnell hinzu, daß es damit auch ein Ende gehabt habe. »Nach Schinkels Tode wirkten seine Schüler Persius, Stüler und Strack in seinem Sinne, freilich ohne an die Genialität des Meisters heranzureichen.« (Muthesius 1902, S. 16; Anderson 1994, S. 55.) Während konservative Kritiker wie Fritz Stahl und Arthur Moeller van den Bruck Potsdam in den veritablen Status eines Kultorts für die vereinigte deutsche Nationalkultur erhoben, sahen sie keinerlei Veranlassung, in Schinkels Meisterwerken nach allgemeinverbindlichen Maßstäben zu suchen. All dies änderte sich ganz plötzlich Mitte der 1920er Jahre. Gezeichnet, aufgemessen, photographiert, analysiert und interpretiert, begann das Werk von Persius ein ganzes Spektrum von Architekten, Kritikern und Historikern zu faszinieren. 1922 forderte der preußische Oberhofbaurat Albert Geyer in einer mehrteiligen Studie über Friedrich Wilhelm IV. als Architekt ein größeres Verständnis für die Rolle von Persius in dem außerordentlichen Kunstwerk, das Potsdam darstelle. Aber das Interesse war erstmals vorwiegend auf den Architekten und nicht auf den königlichen Patron gerichtet, als im Sommer 1925 Persius' Zeichnungen im Architekturmuseum der Technischen Hochschule in Charlottenburg gezeigt wurden, einem Museum, das damals über Generationen hinweg eine permanente Schinkelausstellung angeboten hatte. Die Rezeption der Ausstellung über Persius verweist auf die Rolle, welche die Persius-Rezeption später in den zwei sich entwickelnden und miteinander verbundenen Debatten einnehmen sollte: der Diskussion der Architektur-Avantgarde mit ihrem Ruf nach Abstraktion und organischer Entwicklung einer Gebäudeform nach den Forderungen des Programms sowie der kunsthistorischen Debatte über das Konzept eines »romantischen Klassizismus«.

Während die Ausstellung 1925 Persius' Namen für eine Saison in die Fachpresse brachte, stammten die darauffolgenden Lobpreisungen seines Werkes von zwei jungen, anglophonen Kritikern, die beide Persius zum *missing link* in der Geschichtsschreibung der modernen Architektur erklärten, zum maßgeblichen Wegweiser für die in den kommenden Jahren einzuschlagende Richtung. Der Engländer Peter Fleetwood-Hesketh und der Amerikaner Henry-Russell Hitchcock nahmen in einflußreichen Artikeln für sich in Anspruch, Persius als vergessene Quelle moderner Abstraktion in der Architektur entdeckt zu haben. Die Entdeckung war nicht ganz so eindeutig, wie Fleetwood-Hesketh dies später behauptete, denn schon vorher, im Sommer 1927, hatte der junge englische Architekturstudent auf seiner Entdeckungsreise durch Preußen eine von Geyers Vorlesungen über Friedrich Wilhelm IV. gehört. Aber Fleetwood-Hesketh verlagerte den Schwerpunkt von der Krone auf den Künstler und unterlag dabei vielleicht dem Dilemma des begabten Schülers, der nach einem Weg aus dem Schatten seines Meisters sucht. Zurück in London, publizierten er und sein Bruder Roger zwei großzügig illustrierte Artikel in *The Architects' Journal* über »Ludwig Persius of Potsdam«, in denen sie Persius als den wahren Prototypen für den freien und pittoresken Eklektizismus eines Genies, als den Weg zum modernen Erfindungsreichtum beschrieben. »Es ist immer leicht, seine Gebäude von denen seines Meisters zu unterscheiden. Er betrachtete seine Kunst in einem ganz anderen Licht. Er hatte nichts von dem reformerischen neogriechischen Geist, der sich in so vielen späteren Werken Schinkels zeigt. Gewöhnlich bestehen seine Gebäude aus Bruchstücken aller bekannten Stile. Das vollständige Fehlen historischer Skrupel bewahrt ihn jedoch auch davor, als Wiedererwecker gesehen zu werden. Es war zweifellos vorteilhaft für ihn, in einer Zeit der Wiederaufnahme von Stilen geboren zu sein, denn es bedeutete, daß so viel mehr Stile gewählt werden konnten, aber damit war die Sache erledigt. Bei ihm konnte jede Form neben jeder anderen bestehen, ohne Rücksicht auf den historischen Bezug, solange die Komposition dadurch verbessert wurde. Sein Standpunkt war der eines Landschaftsmalers.« (Fleetwood-Hesketh 1928, S. 80.)

Hitchcock entdeckte Persius auf seinen ausgedehnten Reisen durch Europa in den späten 1920er Jahren nach seiner Graduierung in Harvard. Im Text seines ehrgeizigen jugendlichen Versuchs, den historischen Wurzeln der Moderne gerecht zu werden, in *Modern Architecture, Romanticism and Reintegration* von 1929, wird die Potsdamer Architektur insgesamt als Vorläufer dessen gesehen, was Hitchcock als die »neue Tradition« bezeichnete – die Bauten von Berlage, Behrens und van de Velde –, in einer glänzenden und einflußreichen Unterscheidung von den »neuen Pionieren«, dem Werk von Le Corbusier, Gropius, Mies van der Rohe und J. J. P. Oud in den Niederlanden. Als Hitchcock im Sommer 1930 mit dem jungen Philip Johnson nach Potsdam zurückkehrte, hatte er Persius auf eine Linie mit den neuen Pionieren gebracht. In einem Artikel »The romantic architecture of Potsdam« schrieb er 1931: »Für den Charme von Persius' Werk sprechen seine Anmut, die Zurückhaltung in der Anwendung von Details und die kristalline Klarheit seiner linearen Gestaltung. In den asymmetrischen, eklektischen und zwanglosen Stil der ›italienischen Villa‹ übertrug er die ganze Perfektion der besten klassizistischen Architektur, die häufig im Geist die in völlig anderem Stil gehaltenen Werke von Mies van der Rohe vorwegnimmt, einem der großen deutschen modernen Architekten unserer Tage.« (Hitchcock 1931, S. 46.) Die berühmten Prinzipien des sogenannten Internationalen Stils – Volumen contra Masse, Farbe statt angewandtem Ornament und Regelmäßigkeit statt symmetrischer Komposition – sind alle in Hitchcocks Beschreibungen der Gebäude von Persius vorweggenommen. Und nur ein Jahr später fand Persius seinen Weg in den Text von Hitchcocks und Johnsons einflußreiches Buch *The International Style*, wiederum im Einklang mit der Entwicklung von Mies: »Mies van der Rohe erreichte den neuen Stil zuerst weniger schnell als Gropius«, stellten sie fest, »vor dem Kriege hatte er vereinfacht, geklärt und den einheimischen Stil von Behrens bis zu dem Punkte aufgeheitert, der eine bewußte Inspiration durch Schinkel und Persius nahelegt.« (Hitchcock und Johnson 1932, S. 32.)

Zu dieser Zeit war es bereits klar, daß sich Hitchcock mit dem ganzen Problem des Übergangs vom Barock zur Moderne befaßte, einer Problematik, die ihn und Johnson dazu führte, auf ihrer Reise, die sie 1930 unternahmen, Sigfried Giedion aufzusuchen. Aber wenn irgend etwas für die neue Einschätzung von Persius in

seiner historischen Betrachtung verantwortlich war, dann war es das polemische Argument in dem gerade erschienenen Führer zum romantischen Potsdam, Georg Poensgens *Die Bauten Friedrich Wilhelms IV. in Potsdam*, der Hitchcock und Johnson in diesem Sommer als Führer diente. Nirgendwo fand sich ein schlüssigeres Argument dafür, daß es eine dringende Aufgabe wäre, das unvollendete Projekt der Romantik wiederaufzugreifen – die Ideen der Generation nach Schinkel, die durch den aufkommenden Eklektizismus des späten 19. Jahrhunderts im Keim erstickt worden waren: »Denn obgleich die Ausdrucksformen der einzelnen Kunstarten jener Zeit als Grundlagen der gegenwärtigen Kunst fast allgemein geläufig sind und auch über ihren Ursprung Klarheit herrscht, ist der oberflächliche Betrachter heute eher geneigt, die Unselbständigkeit und Unsachlichkeit der Romantiker tadelnd zu bemerken, als die Ergebnisse ihrer vielseitigen Bestrebungen wohlwollend anzuerkennen. Die ungeistigen und geschmacklosen Erzeugnisse der Gründerzeit ziehen die ihnen vorangegangenen Leistungen auf künstlerischem Gebiet mit in die negative Beurteilung hinein und lassen ihren ausgesprochenen Verdienst in Vergessenheit geraten. Das Wesen der Kunst in der ersten Hälfte des 19. Jahrhunderts liegt vor allem in der Fülle neuer Anregungen, die sie aufnahm, und in der Folgerichtigkeit, mit der sie sie verarbeitete.« (Poensgen 1930, Vorwort.) Poensgen war ein wichtiger Mittler für die Beurteilung von Raum und Komposition in Schinkels und vor allem Persius' Entwurf für das Hofgärtnerhaus und die Römischen Bäder bei Charlottenhof. »Wo Schinkel, der Lehrer und Wegweiser, um 1840 bereits ein wenig veraltet und starr geworden war, ging (Persius) mit seinem Bauherrn neue Wege ...« (Poensgen 1930, S. 8.) Diese Argumentation wurde ein Jahr später bei der großen »Ausstellung Klassizistischer Baukunst« erweitert, die von der Nationalgalerie anläßlich des 150. Todestags von Schinkel veranstaltet wurde. Dort erinnerte Poensgen seine Zeitgenossen an die Bedeutung von Persius für die gegenwärtigen Schwierigkeiten der Architektur. »Die Bauten des heute fast unbekannten Persius lassen sich nicht mehr mit einem Schlagwort (wie Klassizismus) umschreiben, sie haben keine direkten Vorbilder ... Das Sachliche steht immer im Vordergrund, und der Architekt gestattet sich nur dann ... Konzessionen an den romantischen Zeitgeschmack, wenn sie mit der Szenerie der Umgebung und den technischen Erfordernissen unbedingt zusammengehen. ... Nach seinem Tode verfiel alles dem Eklektizismus und der geschmacklichen Barbarei der Gründerjahre.« (Poensgen 1931, S. 43.)

Wenige Jahre später wurden Schinkel und Persius jedoch von den Nationalsozialisten vereinnahmt, von Carl von Lorcks Monographie in der Reihe *Kunstbücher des Volkes*, 1939, bis zu den Artikeln, die später in jenem Jahr in der Illustrierten *Kunst im Dritten Reich* über Gilly und Schinkel erschienen. Darin wurde der ganze Diskurs über die Entstehung der Reformbewegung von Schinkel als Garant für die Authentizität und den Bezug zum Ort sowie die unterbrochene kulturelle Tradition von den Nazi-Propagandisten umgemünzt, begleitet von Photos der neu angefertigten Modelle von Schinkels größeren Werken, ausgeführt im Auftrag von Albert Speer. Der Kunsthistoriker Josef Schmid ließ diesen Trend in der bis heute üppigsten Monographie über Schinkel gipfeln: *Karl Friedrich Schinkel, der Vorläufer neuer deutscher Baugesinnung*, 1943 in Leipzig erschienen. »Erst hundert Jahre nach Schinkel, nach langen Zeiten der Stillosigkeit

und oft wüster Verwahrlosung der Kunst, bekam das deutsche Volk wieder einen großen Baumeister geschenkt: Adolf Hitler.« (Schmid 1943, o. S.)

Doch trotz der Vereinnahmung von Schinkel und Persius durch die Nationalsozialisten wurde ihr Erbe in den 1930er und 1940er Jahren in Amerika weiterhin im Werk deutscher Emigranten, zum Beispiel durch Mies van der Rohe, vertreten, und vielleicht von niemandem mit größerer Originalität als von Walter Curt Behrendt. Im Winter 1934 hielt Behrendt eine Vorlesungsreihe am Dartmouth College, wo er nach Abbruch seiner Berliner Karriere als Interpret der modernen Architektur eine Zuflucht fand. Auf der Suche nach den Wurzeln der Moderne kehrte er wieder ins 19. Jahrhundert zurück. Er beschrieb eine Reihe von Persönlichkeiten, die die großen Herausforderungen der aufkommenden Moderne klar erkannten und in ihrer eigenen Architektur formulierten. Einer davon war Persius, der den Weg zu einer freien Antwort auf programmatische Forderungen wies. Behrendts Persius war nicht nur der Vater der gesamten Tradition organischer Raumplanung, sondern auch der Gottvater von Frank Lloyd Wright: »Der erste Bruch mit dem klassischen Ideal, bis jetzt mit exklusiver Autorität und sorgfältig gesichert, stammte von ... Persius ... Er wies die exzessive Leidenschaft für Symmetrie zurück ... Dies tat er nicht aus ästhetischen Überlegungen, sondern weil diese Leidenschaft, wie er sagte, die Freiheit bei der Entwicklung von nützlichen und komfortablen Innenräumen begrenze ... Er beginnt damit, daß jeder Raum zu dienen habe, und er versucht unerschütterlich, Form und Höhe des Raumes seiner spezifischen Funktion anzupassen. Er hält sich an das Prinzip der freien Gruppierung, um die Räume nach ihren inneren Bezügen zu arrangieren. Seine Pläne sind auf die günstigste Ausrichtung zur Sonne hin konzipiert und darauf, die Räume sowohl auf die nähere Umgebung des Gartens als auch auf den weiteren Blick in die umgebende Landschaft zu öffnen. Die Gebäude schmiegen sich an die Topographie des Ortes an, sie sind in intimem Kontakt mit dem Boden entwickelt ... mit ihrer heiteren Anmut sind bereits einige Ideen vorweggenommen, die später, voll ausgereift, im Werk von Frank Lloyd Wright realisiert werden.« (Behrendt 1937, S. 43/44.) Wrights frühe Prärie-Periode, durch die Publikation von Wasmuth 1911 berühmt gemacht, wurde nun praktisch als Reifungsprozeß des Projekts angesehen, das 1845 mit Persius' allzu frühem Tod in Potsdam abgebrochen worden war.

In einem Fries Otto Geyers, der die Treppenhalle einer der letzten Bauten Stülers, die Nationalgalerie, schmückt, die er zusammen mit Strack entworfen hatte, wird das 19. Jahrhundert als Apotheose der deutschen Kultur und Kunst gefeiert. Eine ebensolche Anerkennung wurde Stüler in der kritischen Geschichtsschreibung über die preußische Architektur des 19. Jahrhunderts jedoch lange Zeit nicht zuteil. Er genoß nie dieselbe Erhebung zum Vorläufer der Moderne, wie sie Schinkel und Persius als Ausgangspunkte für Ursprung und Neubeginn ständig erfuhren. (Wullen 2002, S. 36.) Und dies trotz der Tatsache, daß er in vielen seiner Gebäude, besonders dem Neuen Museum, technische Neuerungen mit neuen Materialien einführte, mit Gewölbeüberspannungen, wie sie von Schinkel nie erprobt worden waren. In zahllosen Kirchen vertrat er die nach 1830 von vielen geteilte Überzeugung, daß die stilistische Vereinnahmung des Rundbogenstils auf eine moderne Architektur des 19. Jahrhunderts verweise, die über historische Imitation hinausgehe. Als Stüler im Jahr 1865 starb, war er auf der Höhe seines Schaffens, und sein Tod wurde als das Ende einer Ära in der Berliner Architektur angesehen. »Was soll nun werden?«, fragte der Herausgeber der *Zeitschrift für Bauwesen*. Aber 35 Jahre später kehrte die Presse anläßlich der Feier zu seinem hundertsten Geburtstag zur Stüler-Frage zurück. Nahezu alle stimmten darin überein, daß der Verfall seiner Anerkennung und Wertschätzung ebenso bemerkenswert sei wie die nahezu zeitlose Gunst, die Schinkel entgegengebracht wurde. »In den kunstgeschichtlichen Werken wird seine schöpferische Thätigkeit meist mit wenigen Zeilen abgethan und gegenüber derjenigen Schinkels als schwächliches Epigonenthum bezeichnet«, notierte K. E. O. Fritsch in einer Rede vor dem Architekten-Verein, den Stüler gegründet hatte. (Fritsch 1900, S. 58–60.) In einem defensiven Ton suchte Fritsch nach dem kreativen Wert vieler Stülerscher Schöpfungen, aber wie viele andere argumentierte auch er, daß dieses beträchtliche Talent weitgehend von einer übergroßen Nachgiebigkeit gegenüber seinem Herrn, Friedrich Wilhelm IV., geschmälert worden sei. Diese Ansicht machte sich der einflußreiche amerikanische Architekturhistoriker Hitchcock schon 1928 zu eigen, als er, in einer freien Wiedergabe von Muthesius, feststellte, daß Stüler, den er inkorrekterweise als Schinkelschüler bezeichnete, »wenig von dem Genius seines Meisters besaß.« (Hitchcock 1928, S. 38.) Noch 1958, als das Innere des Neuen Museums unzugänglich war, urteilte Hitchcock, daß die äußere Schlichtheit des Neuen Museums als Beweis für den rapiden Verfall rationalistischer griechischer Standards diene, der in den Jahrzehnten (nach Schinkels Wirken) in den Arbeiten von Schinkels fähigsten Schülern zu erkennen sei. (Hitchcock 1958, S. 61.) Diese Sicht gründete einmal mehr in der Bewertung von Georg Poensgen, der ein gleichlautendes Urteil über Stüler abgab: »Als dann auch Persius, viel zu früh, im Jahr 1845 starb, trat an seine Stelle August Stüler, gleichfalls ein Schinkelschüler, der sich jedoch im Gegensatz zu Persius niemals von den Vorbildern des gemeinsamen Lehrers freimachen konnte und dessen Tätigkeit sich lediglich auf eine geschmackvolle Vollendung der ihm hinterlassenen Projekte beschränkte. Er überlebte den König um einige Jahre, und mit seinem Tode (1865) fand eine Epoche europäischer Baukunst ihr Ende ...« (Poensgen 1930, S. 8.)

Eine faszinierende Schicksalswende findet sich sodann in der Entwicklung der Kommentare des Kritikers Karl Scheffler über Stüler. In einem Artikel über Behrens in *Die Zukunft* schrieb Scheffler 1907, daß Behrens' Arbeitsweise direkt zu der großen letzten Architekturperiode, »zu der Zeit von Schinkel, Strack und Stüler«, zurückkehre. (Anderson 2001, S. 116.) Wieder über Behrens schreibend, stellte Scheffler 1913 in *Die Architektur der Großstadt* fest, daß jeder, der 50 Jahre vorher nach Berlin gereist sei, von den großen, monumentalen Gebäuden geredet habe: Brandenburger Tor, Schauspielhaus oder Museum am Lustgarten. Heute würden sich die Freunde moderner Baukunst lieber den Nutzbauten Berlins zuwenden: etwa Messels Warenhaus und Behrens' Bauten für die AEG. Dieser Umschlag des Interesses signalisierte den Wandel des Interesses in jener Zeit. »Es liegt nicht an den Künstlern, nicht daran, daß Messel und Behrens andersgeartete Baumeistertalente sind wie Gentz, Langhans, Schinkel, Stüler oder Wäsemann. Im Gegenteil, diese beiden Architekten und die ihrer Gesinnung sind recht eigentlich Traditionsträger, sie gehören zu den legitimen Nachfolgen jener führenden Talente der Berliner Bauschule« (Scheffler 1913, S. 128/129.) Aber

dann, 1939, tadelte Scheffler Schinkel und seine Schüler scharf, wohl als eine Reaktion auf ihre polemische Vereinnahmung durch die Nationalsozialisten, daß sie der Architektur erlaubt hätten, in grandiosen und grundlosen Phantasien zu gipfeln. »Der Baumeister klassischer Epochen war stets bestrebt, sich dem groß Originalen seiner Zeit, dem allgemeinen Stilwillen einzuordnen; der moderne Architekt begann, historische Bauformen ohne inneren Zwang zu wiederholen, und strengte sich nur an, es in einer Weise zu tun, die ihm allein nicht original sein konnte. Fehlten die Bauaufträge, so lebte die Begabung sich am Zeichentisch, im Atelier, auf dem Papier aus. Es trat eine willkürliche, genialisch sich gebärdende Entwurfsarchitektur in Erscheinung. Bereits bei Friedrich Gilly und Schinkel begann es. Stadtpläne oder Großstadtkorrekturen von riesenhaften Ausmaßen wurden ersonnen und Phantasiearchitekturen, die Wunschträume waren.« (Scheffler 1939, S. 110.) Im selben Jahr enthüllte Speer, anläßlich des fünfzigsten Geburtstags von Hitler am 20. April 1939, das Modell des großen Triumphbogens, das sogenannte Bauwerk T. Dieses Monumentalprojekt verdammte einen von Stülers zahlreichen Kirchenbauten zum Abriß, die St. Matthäuskirche im Tiergarten, die genau auf der großen, von Speer geplanten Achse stand. Niemand setzte sich für sie ein, auch wenn 1943 einer von Stülers Nachkommen im eleganten nationalsozialistischen Kunstmagazin *Kunst im Deutschen Reich* eine Verherrlichung Stülers schrieb. (Müller-Stüler, 1943.)

Obwohl das Pfarrhaus von St. Matthäus schon 1939 abgerissen wurde, blieb die Kirche stehen, weil die Belastungen des Krieges den Fortschritt der Baupläne von Speer und Hitler verzögerten. In den letzten Tagen des Krieges bis auf die Außenmauern ausgebrannt, wurde sie von den Architekten Jürgen Emmrich und H. Patek zwischen 1956 und 1960 wiederaufgebaut, nach Eva Börsch-Supan aufgrund der weithin verbreiteten, allerdings fälschlichen Annahme, es handele sich um einen Schinkelbau. (Börsch-Supan und Müller-Stüler, 1997, S. 532.) Mit dem nur wenige Jahre später erfolgten Bau der Neuen Nationalgalerie von Mies van der Rohe, dem ersten Gebäude des geplanten Kulturforums, welches das einst dicht bebaute Tiergartenviertel im Zentrum Berlins in eine Landschaft aus modernen Baudenkmälern verwandelt hat, wurde Stülers wiederaufgebaute Kirche zu einer Ikone des aus den Trümmern wiedererstandenen Berlins. Mies selbst wählte diesen Standort, und obgleich sein Tempel auf einem Podium lange als ein Stück autonomer Architektur gepriesen wurde, machte er weitergehende Pläne, um die Rastergeometrie seines neuen Bauwerks mit den Hauptachsen der wiedererrichteten Kirche aus dem 19. Jahrhundert, eines der strengsten und abstraktesten Kirchenentwürfe Stülers, in Einklang zu bringen. Seit Fertigstellung des Museums Ende der 1960er Jahre zeigt eine der berühmtesten Photographien die Glaswand und frei stehenden stählernen Doppel-T-Träger des Mies-Baus im Kontrast zur erhaltenen Bebauung des 19. Jahrhunderts, verkörpert durch Stülers wiederaufgebaute Kirche. Obgleich diese bekannte Photographie 1968 auf dem Umschlag der *Bauwelt* anläßlich der Vollendung von Mies' erstem und einzigem Nachkriegsbau in Berlin erschien, geriet doch der Name Stülers gegenüber dem Schinkels einmal mehr ins Hintertreffen: Ulrich Conrads erwähnte in seiner Besprechung des Gebäudes Mies' eigene Behauptung von 1961, daß man alles, was man über Architektur wissen müsse, aus dem Studium von Schinkels Altem Mu-

seum lernen könne. Conrads schloß seine Kritik mit dem Hinweis auf den Bezugspunkt der zentralen Achse der Stülerschen Kirche mit folgenden Worten: «Ich kenne keinen Bau, der ruhiger, abgeklärter, statischer wäre als dieser. Er ist Mies van der Rohes entschiedenster Gang Arm in Arm mit Schinkel.» (Conrads 1968, S. 1210.) Die Redakteure der *Bauwelt* begleiteten ihre umfassende Analyse des Bauwerks mit einem Zitat aus Schinkels später Veröffentlichung über Orianda, um die Tatsache zu rechtfertigen, das Mies' Ästhetik und Wagemut von Schinkels Werk vorbereitet wurden, das den Historismus überwand, und dies in einer Art und Weise, wie sie nur wenige Stüler zugebilligt hätten: »Die Mitte des Kaiserlichen Hofes füllt ein Unterbau, auf dessen Plattform sich ein vermittels großer Spiegelscheiben fast durchsichtiger Pavillon in Tempelform erhebt ... Dieser Tempel war als Krönung des ganzen Baues, um die einfachen Linien griechischer Architektur malerisch zu unterbrechen, ganz unentbehrlich.« (*Bauwelt*, 16. September 1968, S. 3.)

Während Stülers Bauwerke wirklich am Wendepunkt der neueren deutschen Geschichte standen, vom Turm der Kirche St. Matthäus im Herzen des Kulturforums zum zentralen Neuen Museum und zu den Projekten der Museumsinsel, beides Objekte des UNESCO-Welterbes und Kernstücke der Kulturpolitik des wiedervereinigten Berlins, wurde also Stülers Name nie in der ideologisch aufgeladenen Weise kodiert, wie das bei Schinkel und Persius im Zuge der Erneuerung der Architektur geschah. Darin liegt eine gewisse Ironie, weil Stüler seine ganze Karriere der Aufgabe gewidmet hatte, ebendiese von Schinkel aufgeworfenen Fragen zu lösen: wie die Architektur über den historischen Bezug hinausgehen und Verbindungen mit den Richtungen der historischen Entwicklung knüpfen könne, sowohl in seinen Rundbogen-Bauten als auch in der von Schinkel beharrlich vertretenen Überzeugung, daß sich neue Formen entwickeln würden, wenn man nur die Möglichkeiten von Eisen und neuen Materialien, zum Beispiel Terrakotta, als integrale Bestandteile einer sich entwickelnden architektonischen Sprache beachtete.

Barry Bergdoll
»... the last great, comprehensive genius that architecture has produced.« Karl Friedrich Schinkel and his pupils in the eyes of the modern movement

Few architectural developments of the 19th century sponsored a more shifting reception than that of the Berlin school of Karl Friedrich Schinkel and his immediate followers, most prominently among them the short-lived Ludwig Persius and the prolific Friedrich August Stüler. Now that the work of this trio, who set the tone for Berlin architecture for over half a century, has been collected by the reconnaissance missions of Hillert Ibbeken, we have before us the evidence in black and white of a decades-long stylistic tradition that lent international recognition to Berlin by the mid-19th century as a city possessed of a distinctive architectural culture, one that could rival Paris with it's Beaux-Arts tradition which also was to enjoy an international influence. By the early 20th century as the heritage of the École des Beaux-Arts came under attack for its academicism, just as the tradition of the English Gothic Revival did for its historicism, the legacy of Schinkel and his followers was often exempt from this sweeping rejection of 19th-century architectural culture. For Hermann Muthesius, diagnosing in his 1902 Stilarchitektur und Baukunst the ills of eclecticism that had beset much of 19th-century architecture Schinkel was »the last great, comprehensive genius that architecture has produced« (Muthesius 1994, p. 55), a clear point of departure for the reform of modern design practice. Muthesius considered Berlin a great exception in the development of 19th-century architecture, the Schinkel school having been a veritable bulwark against stylistic eclecticism and superficial.

This was a radical reversal of the reception of their work during their lifetimes. For in the mid-19th century both the monumental classical public works of Schinkel and Stüler and the asymmetrical villa perfected by Schinkel and Persius enjoyed international influence as sophisticated models of the adoption of historical styles to modern uses. Particularly in the international fashion for the asymmetrical Italian villa at mid century the influence of the Berlin school was wide-spread. Schinkel gained international repute through the engravings of his Sammlung Architektonischer Entwürfe, which found its way as far north as Scotland where Alexander »Greek« Thomson not only took inspiration from Schinkel's rigorous raster-like fenestration in some of his churches and commercial blocks, but also from the taught picturesque villa massing of Schinkel and Persius's Court Gardener's House in his masterful Holmwood Villa, Glasgow of 1857/58, recently restored. A few years later Thomson donated his copy of Schinkel's great portfolio to the Glasgow Architectural Society. But while Schinkel's influence is palpable in the details of several of Thomson's severe renderings of a modern neo-Greek, notably at Holmwood, it was thoroughly synthesized with long-standing native British taste and tradition for the picturesque Italianate villa – one that can be traced back at least to the work of John Nash in the opening years of the century. (Stamp 1998.)

The influence of Persius's Potsdam villas – down to the level of details – is unmistakable in the Alsop House (1838–40) in Wesleyan, Connecticut, often attributed to the architect Ithiel Town, but this is a rare case of un-adulterated influence. By the mid-1850s – when American architect Henry van Brunt noted the wide-spread influence of German architectural periodicals on American architectural design – the volumes of those two great compendia of the new asymmetrical compositional modes and abstraction of vernacular detail perfected in Berlin-Potsdam, the Architektonisches Album (1840–62), and most particularly the Architektonisches Skizzenbuch (1852–66), were widely consulted in fashionable New York architectural offices. Copies of these, and of the Entwürfe zu Kirchen, Pfarr- und Schulbauten, which was to have a noted influence on American Protestant church design, were to be found not only in the Astor Library in New York but as standard sources in some of the most prominent New York offices – including those of P. B. Wight, Edward T. Potter, and probably Russell Sturgis. (Landau 1983, p. 273.) The Schinkel-Persius-Stüler tradition was an undeniable ingredient in the picturesque massing and casual spatial planning associated with the development of American resort architecture, notably in the early Newport villas of Richard Morris Hunt and his followers, a development long seen as the essential starting point for the exploration of new planning and compositional techniques in the early work of Frank Lloyd Wright.

The transformation of the Schinkel tradition from compositional source to a polemical stance for authenticity in expression and for transcending historical imagery was also promoted in America, even before it became a veritable leitmotif of the Reform generation in German modernism around the turn of the century. It was above all in Chicago not only a cradle of American modern architecture, but also one of the most Germanically-stamped cultures in 19th-century America, that Schinkel's legacy actually became a part of the local professional discussion. Only four years after Stüler's death, the German émigré Frederick Baumann (1826–1921), who from his arrival in Chicago in 1850 was a great contributor to the technical innovations that led to the development of the high-rise skyscraper (notably independent footings which could be traced back at least to Schinkel's Altes Museum as a Prussian solution to building on sandy soil), began to celebrate actively the legacy of Schinkel's search for tectonic purity as a guiding force in the forging of an architectural present. In 1869 Baumann published an abridged translation of Friedrich Adler's »Schinkelfestrede« of the same year, the first of several texts that would appear in Chicago's architectural periodicals celebrating Schinkel as a precursor of modern architecture, indeed as the inventor of the architectural sobriety and matter-of-factness that could embody the pragmatic spirit of business building to prevail in the development of Chicago's downtown. Adler had pointed especially to the freedom from historical reference of Schinkel's Bauakademie and admired its »chaste severity, sober beauty ... And engaging originality« which made it resemble »a seed which promises further organic development«. (Adler 1869, p. 199.) Anticipating by nearly two decades the theme that Muthesius would develop, Adler and by adoption Baumann coined the notion of Schinkel as the forerunner of honest and »sachlich« building equipped to deal with the realities of materials and of modern spatial needs with little sense of nostalgia for the revival of historical style.

The opening years of the 20th century in Germany were marked by an intense renewal of interest in Schinkel's architecture, spearheaded by a faith that by renew-ing with the last glowing moment of Prussian classicism, the path towards a genuine cultural expression for modern Germany might be illuminated. Perhaps no one voiced as clearly the sense in which Schinkel was thought to open the path for an escape from historicist culture than Adolf Loos, who in 1910 said of Schinkel: »We have forgotten him, may the light of this stellar figure also fall upon the coming generation of our architects.« (Loos 1992, p. 317.) Perhaps this was true in Loos's Vienna, but, as the critic Paul Westheim noted in a 1913 key article, »Schinkel und die Gegenwart«, there had scarcely been a moment in the German capital in which Schinkel had fallen from prominence. The danger, Westheim felt, was not that architects had forgotten Schinkel but that his memory had been defamed in pastiche: »But is it more than architectonic mannerism what is exhibited on Berlin's streets as the latest fashion under the label ›Schinkel‹? (Westheim 1913, p. B 83.)«, he quipped.

By 1913 Westheim joined a chorus of voices, voices moreover that spanned the ideological divisions of the current debates. A whole generation, inspired by the joint calls of Friedrich Nietzsche's attack on historicism and of the continued enthusiasm for Julius Langbehn's 1890 Rembrandt als Erzieher looked to Schinkel as part of what Paul Mebe's in 1908 labeled »Architecture and handicraft in the last century of its natural development«. Mebes's Um 1800 published for the first time in 1908, but reissued several times by 1925, was a major vehicle. Mebes's aim was to turn the spotlight on the anonymous architecture of the last turn-of-the century as an anchor in the confusing storm of current debate in order to confront what he characterizes as a crisis of authenticity in modernizing bourgeois culture. For him it was sufficient to stroll through any of the new districts of German cities to realize the full urgency of the crisis, which was not limited to the total loss of meaning in architectural expression but also of a whole culture of know-how which is as much the heritage of a culture as it's monuments. For Mebes, as for Muthesius, one of the great dangers of the acceleration of the industrial revolution was the capacity to imitate styles without understanding the constructional systems and the societal values that were inherent to their forms. The solution is for architects to renew with the broken tradition of architecture at the very beginning of the 19th century. For the most part this is embodied in unpretentious vernacular buildings, but Schinkel's is virtually the only name that Mebes allows into the compendium of over several hundred exemplars of a sensibility of no clear and unpretentious »bürgerlich« building of the late 18th and early 19th century. By 1918, when he published a second expanded edition, Mebes had coupled with Walter Curt Behrendt, who would emerge as one of the great protagonists of Bauhaus modernism in the 1920s. Behrendt noted that the generalizing interest in neo-Classicism is poised to become a new sort of »international style« to such an extent that »there must be something on the spiritual plane which unites contemporary architecture with that of the period around 1800 to such an extent that we find there a natural departure point for confronting the challenges of our modern world«. (Mebes 1918.)

No one fulfilled this program more fully before World War I than Peter Behrens, in whose Neu-Babelsberg studio Ludwig Mies, Charles Edouard Jeanneret (the future Le Corbusier), and Walter Gropius all briefly worked in the years between 1908 and 1912. Even before Behrens had left Düsseldorf for Berlin in 1907 to accept the famous commission to redesign the buildings, products, and corporate image of the German AEG, the art critic Julius Meier-Graefe, a booster, celebrated Behren's underlying classicism and wished it could be generalized to sponsor a wider renewal of architecture. »Would it not be possible to build such that nothing of the form, but only the cool spirit of the Greeks, so worthy of devotion, would arise?« (Anderson, 2001, p. 118.) Fritz Schumacher, who had published a crucial essay on tradition and innovation in 1901, recalled years later a visit to Behrens in Neu-Babelsberg and noted that Behrens had taken him to see »his beloved small Schinkel buildings.« (Schumacher 1944, p. 22, cited in Anderson 2001, p. 116.) The pinnacle of Behren's engagement with the Berlin classical tradition, and indeed the highpoint of the critical celebration of Schinkel in Berlin architectural circles in general, came in 1911/12. In that year Behrens had simultaneously under construction two major buildings whose formal and spatial qualities relate directly to the idea of emulating Schinkel as a method of inventing an architectural language within a tradition rather than in any direct imitation of a whole or part of one of Schinkel's designs. In both the Wiegand house in Berlin-Dahlem and the Mannesmann administration building in Düsseldorf, Behrens looked to Schinkel's quest for a new abstracted and elemental ordering system, related to the orders but free of any literal classicalism. In the Wiegand house Schinkel's monumental quest for an elemental ordering with the tartan like interweaving of interior and exterior spaces, of house and garden, that Schinkel and Persius had achieved at the Court Gardener's House at Schloss Charlottenhof at Sanssouci (1829–33). As early as 1861 Stüler had celebrated Charlottenhof as »the most original project that has ever been devised, in the spirit of the past times from the standpoint of present-day architecture«. (Stüler 1861, p. 19.) In a review of the Wiegand house in the influential *Innendekoration*, the architectural critic Robert Breuer saw Behrens as poised between the past and future of architecture, at once a »seer of form« and »the fulfillment of Schinkel.« (Breuer 1913, cited in Anderson 2001, p. 119.) As the buildings were nearing completion the first monograph on Schinkel since the 19th century was published by the great Berlin publisher Wasmuth, signed by Fritz Stahl, the newly adopted pseudonym of the critic Siegfried Lilienthal: »This text is the result of a conviction that Karl Friedrich Schinkel is the up and coming man of our architecture, and that for architects there is no more pressing matter than to know him and his works well. The renown and influence that he enjoyed in his lifetime, and even fifty years after his death, are nothing in comparison to the renown and influence that he is going to have. Like all geniuses he was a century ahead of his time. Those who lived with him and immediately after him could only really comprehend a part of him. Before we can grasp his whole being to its very essence we still have a lot to learn. Anyone who knows how late it was that Germans were ready for Goethe will not be surprised that we are only now ready for Schinkel.« (Stahl, 1911, p. 3.) In 1927 Behrens himself, giving that year's »Schinkelfestrede« under the title »Zum Problem der technischen und tektonischen Beziehungen«, spoke in admiration of Le Corbusier before concluding that »in this a modern spirit speaks that commits itself to idealism, and in this we are returned to the man who sought beauty and founded

Sachlichkeit, Carl Friedrich Schinkel«. (Posener 1981, p. 290.)

Although Mies had followed this program to the letter in such pre-war buildings as the Perls house of 1911 in Zehlendorf, so unmistakably indebted to the royal pavilion at Charlottenburg, Mies nonetheless went unnoticed in the summary of the Schinkel revival offered by Paul Westheim in 1913 in which he had called for architect's to penetrate to the essence of Schinkel's sense of from rather than the outward traces of his style. Fourteen years later, in an article devoted to Mies van der Rohe, the first survey ever published of the emerging avant-garde architect's work, Westheim returned to the subject of Schinkel's persistent influence in a much-changed Berlin architectural scene. Although by then Mies had radically restyled both himself and in his architecture by 1927, when he was concluding work as director of the Weissenhof housing exhibition at Stuttgart, Westheim returned to Mies's arrival in Berlin in 1905 – the Berlin of the Schinkel revival – to explore and to argue that while »Mies ... has nothing left of a so-called Schinkel style«, he was nonetheless »one of the most gifted, because one of the most primordial of Schinkel pupils« (Westheim 1927, p. 57) precisely because he fulfilled what Westheim had already called for in 1913, not a pastiche of Schinkel's formal repertoire but rather an engagement with Schinkel's »astounding feeling for masses, relationships, rhythms and fitness to form«. (Westheim 1927, p. 53.) In 1927 Westheim picked up with this analysis: »Mies, who drew close to Schinkel and at first, as usual, worked through him with a certain formal language discovered for himself behind the classical Schinkel, the other Schinkel, who was an eminently objective (*sachlich*) architect. That is what makes Schinkel's Altes Museum such an excellent museum building and what makes the Nationalgalerie of a so-called Schinkel pupil, for whom style and not substance was decisive, such a hopeless botch-job of a museum building.« (Westheim 1927, p. 56.)

If in *Stilarchitektur* Muthesius had called Schinkel »the last great, comprehensive genius that architecture has produced«, he was quick to add that it stopped there: »After Schinkel's death his students Persius, Stüler and Strack practiced in his manner, obviously without attaining the genius of the master.« (Anderson 1994, p. 55, after Muthesius 1902, p. 16.) While conservative critics such as Fritz Stahl and Arthur Moeller van den Broek elevated Potsdam to the veritable status of a cult site for a unified German national culture, they saw no need to look beyond Schinkel's masterpieces for standards. All this changed quite suddenly in the mid 1920s. Sketched, measured, photographed, analyzed, and interpreted, Persius's work came to fascinate a spectrum of architects, critics, and historians. In 1922 Prussian Oberhofbaurat Albert Geyer called for a greater understanding of the role of Persius in the extraordinary work of art that was Potsdam in a multi-part study on Friedrich Wilhelm IV as architect. But the spotlight was focused primarily on the architect rather than the royal patron for the first time only in the summer 1925 exhibition of Persius's drawings at the Architekturmuseum of the Technische Hochschule in Charlottenburg, a museum which had by that time for generations offered a permanent exhibition of Schinkel. The reception of the Persius exhibition points to the role Persius's reception would have in two interlocked and emerging debates: the ongoing debates of the architectural avant-gardes with their

claims for abstraction and organic development of a building form from the necessities of program, and the art-historical debate over the concept of »romantic classicism«.

While the 1925 exhibition put Persius's name in the specialized press for a season, the next celebrations of his work came from two young Anglophone critics, both of whom were to proclaim Persius as the missing link in the developmental history of modern architecture and as a vital signpost for the path to follow in the coming years. The Englishman Peter Fleetwood-Hesketh and the American Henry-Russell Hitchcock both claimed in influential articles to have discovered Persius as a forgotten source of modern abstraction in architecture. The discovery was not quite so complete as Fleetwood-Hesketh later claimed, for earlier in the summer of 1927, on his voyage of discovery to Prussia, the young English architecture student had attended one of Geyer's lectures on Friedrich Wilhelm IV. But Fleetwood-Hesketh shifted the focus from the crown to the artist, identifying perhaps also with the dilemma of how a gifted pupil makes his way out from under the shadow of his master. Back in London, he and his brother Roger published two extensively illustrated articles in *The Architects' Journal* on »Ludwig Persius of Potsdam,« in which they describe Persius as the veritable prototype for a free and picturesque eclecticism of genius as the path to modern invention: »It is always easy to distinguish his buildings from those of his master. He looked upon his art in quite a different light. He had none of the reforming neo-Grec spirit which displays itself in so much of Schinkel's later work. His buildings were usually made up of fragments of every known style. Yet his complete lack of historical scruple must prevent him from being called a revivalist. It was no doubt an advantage to him to have been born in a revivalist age because it meant so many more styles to choose from but there the matter ended. With him any shape went in beside any other shape, without regard for the historical origin of either, so long as the composition was thereby improved. His outlook was that of a landscape painter.« (Fleetwood-Hesketh 1928, p. 80.)

Hitchcock discovered Persius during extensive European travels in the late 1920s after his graduation from Harvard. In the text of his ambitious youthful attempt to make sense of the historical roots of modernism: *Modern Architecture: Romanticism and Reintegration* of 1929, Potsdam architecture as a whole is seen as a forerunner of what Hitchcock dubbed the »new tradition« – Berlage, Behrens, and van de Velde – in a famous and influential distinction with the »new pioneers«, the work of Le Corbusier, Gropius, Mies van der Rohe, and J. J. P. Oud in the Netherlands. By the time Hitchcock returned to Potsdam in summer 1930 with the young Philip Johnson, Hitchcock had realigned Persius with the new pioneers. In a 1931 article on »The romantic architecture of Potsdam«, he wrote: »For the charm of Persius's work was its delicacy, the restraint in the use of detail and the crystalline clarity of its linear design. He carried over in the asymmetrical, eclectic and informal manner of the ›Italian Villa‹ all the perfection of the Greek Revival at its best, which often seems to fore-shadow in spirit the work in a wholly different style of Mies van der Rohe, one of the great German modernists of our own day.« (Hitchcock 1931, p. 46.) The famous principles of the so-called International Style – volume versus mass, color rather than applied decoration, and regularity rather than symmetrical composition – are all anticipated in Hitchcock's descriptions of Persius's buildings. And just one year later Persius found his way into the text of Hitchcock and Johnson's seminal *The International Style*, again aligned with Mies's evolution: »Mies van der Rohe advanced toward the new style less rapidly at first than Gropius«, they noted. »Before the War he had simplified, clarified, and lightened the domestic style of Behrens to the point that suggests conscious inspiration from Schinkel and Persius.« (Hitchcock and Johnson 1932, p. 32.)

By this time it was clear that Hitchcock saw himself as taking up the whole problem of the transition from the Baroque to the modern age, a problematic that led him and Johnson to seek out Sigfried Giedion during their travels in 1930. But if anything accounts for the new importance of Persius in his historical thinking it was the polemical argument embedded in the newly printed guidebook to romantic Potsdam, Georg Poensgen's *Die Bauten Friedrich Wilhelms IV. in Potsdam*, which served as Hitchcock and Johnson's guide that summer. Nowhere was to be found more succinctly the argument that the urgent task was to reconnect with the unfinished project of romanticism, the project of the generation after Schinkel, which had been nipped in the bud by the rampant eclecticism of the late 19th century: »And even though the expressive forms of individual types of art of that period are pervasively the foundations of contemporary art and reign over its clarity, today's superficial observer has a tendency to notice and fault the lack of independence and non-objectiveness (*Unsachlichkeit*) of the romantics, rather than recognizing the wholesome effects of its multi-faceted efforts. The spiritless and tasteless works of the period of unification (*Gründerzeit*) brought earlier artistic accomplishments along with them into a negative spotlight and caused these earlier accomplishments to be forgotten. The essence of art in the first half of the 19th century was above all the fulfillment of the new tasks that it took on, and the logical ways in which it worked through them.« (Poensgen, 1930, preface.) Poensgen situated a fundamental threshold in the whole attitude toward space and composition in Schinkel and particularly in Persius's designs for the Court Gardener's House and Roman Baths complex at Charlottenhof. »While Schinkel had been the teacher and the path breaker, around 1840 this was already getting to be a bit out-dated, and Persius began, with his patron, to follow a new direction ...« (Poensgen 1930, S. 8.) The argument was extended a year later in the great »Ausstellung klassizistischer Baukunst« (Exhibition of neoclassical architecture) organized by the Nationalgalerie for the 150th anniversary of Schinkel's death. There Poensgen reminded his contemporaries of the relevance of Persius to contemporary dilemmas in architecture. »The buildings of Persius, today almost totally unknown, can no longer be subsumed under a single label like neo-Classicism; they have no direct prototype ... The objective is always in the foreground and the architect only makes ... concessions to the period's romantic tastes when he had absolutely to work with the local setting and with technical necessities ... After Persius's death everything collapsed into the eclecticism and the tasteless barbarity of the years around German unification.« (Poensgen 1931, p. 43.)

Within a few years however Schinkel and Persius would be coopted by the National Socialists. From Carl von Lorck's monograph in the series *Kunstbücher des*

Volkes in 1939 to the articles that began to appear later that year in the glossy *Kunst im Dritten Reich* on Gilly and Schinkel, these complete with photographs of the newly completed models of Schinkel's major works executed under Albert Speer's direction, the whole discourse of the reform movement's discovery of Schinkel as a guarantor of authenticity and a connection to place and a cultural tradition interrupted was redirected by Nazi propagandists. The art historian Josef Schmid culminated this trend in the most lavish monograph on Schinkel to date, *Karl Friedrich Schinkel. Der Vorläufer neuer deutscher Baugesinnung*, published in Leipzig in 1943. »Only one hundred years after Schinkel, after a long period of stylelessness and often desolate loss of a genuine artistic spirit, the German people have once again been sent a great building master: Adolf Hitler.« (Schmid 1943, n. p.)

But despite the Nazi cooption of Schinkel and Persius, their legacy continued to be developed in America throughout the 1930s and 1940s, in the work of German émigrés, including Mies van der Rohe in building, and perhaps none with greater originality than Walter Curt Behrendt. In the winter of 1934 Behrendt delivered a series of lectures at Dartmouth College, where he found refuge from his aborted career in Berlin as an interpreter of the modern cause. In seeking the roots of modernism he returned once again to the 19th century, and he outlined there a series of individuals who had been able to see clearly to the greatest challenges that faced emerging modernity in formulating its own architecture. Persius was one of those who led the way in responding frankly to new programmatic needs. Behrendt's Persius is not only the father of the whole tradition of organic spatial planning but the godfather of Frank Lloyd Wright: »The first break with the classical ideal, as yet of exclusive authority and carefully guarded, was made by ... Persius ... He rejected the excessive passion for symmetry ... This he did not for esthetic reasons, but because that passion, he said, restricted freedom in developing a useful and comfortable interior ... He starts from the use each room has to serve, and he steadfastly tries to adapt the form and height of the room to its specific function. He keeps to the principle of free grouping, in order to arrange the rooms according to their inner relationship. His plans are designed to provide the most favorable exposure to the sun, and to open to the rooms both the near prospect of the garden and the distant view of the surrounding landscape. ... The buildings clinging to the topographical contour of the site, are developed in intimate contact with the soil ... with their serene grace, there are already anticipated some of the ideas which much later, grown to full maturity, were realized in the work of Frank Lloyd Wright.« (Behrendt 1937, pp. 43/44.) Wright's early Prairie period, made famous by its 1911 publication by Wasmuth, is seen now practically as a maturation of a project cut short in 1845 with Persius's premature death in Potsdam.

In the great celebration of the 19th century as the apotheosis of the rise of German culture and art in Otto Geyer's great frieze that adorns the stairhall of one of Stüler's last projects, the Nationalgalerie (designed with Strack), this equal status would not be long shared in the critical fortune of the historiography of Prussian 19th-century architecture. Stüler would never enjoy the elevation to a forerunner of modernity that kept Schinkel's and Persius's names ever refreshed as points of origin and new departure. (Wullen 2002, p. 36.) And this de-

spite the fact that in many of his buildings – the Neues Museum in particular – he took technical innovation with new materials and vaulting types to greater lengths that had ever been explored by Schinkel, and in countless churches explored the conviction held by many after 1830 that the stylistic amalgam of the *Rundbogenstil* might point to a modern architecture for the 19th century that transcended historical imitation.

At the time of his death in 1865 Stüler was at the height of his powers, and his death was seen as the end of an era in Berlin architecture, »What now?«, asked the editor of the *Zeitschrift für Bauwesen*. But by the time the press returned to the question of Stüler again, 35 years later in celebrating the 100th anniversary of his birth, nearly all agreed that his fall from his favor and estimation was every bit as remarkable as the nearly perennial favor accorded Schinkel. »In art historical writings his creative activity is usually dismissed in a few lines, and in juxtaposition with Schinkel he is classed as a weak epigone«, noted K. E. O. Fritsch in a speech before the very Architekten-Verein of which Stüler had been a founding member. (Fritsch, 1900, p. 58–60.) In a defensive tone Fritsch sought out the creative virtues of many of Stüler's creations, but argued – like many others – that his considerable talent had largely been diminished by an over willingness to concede to his patron, Friedrich Wilhelm IV. This was the view that the influential American architectural historian Hitchcock adopted as early as 1928, when paraphrasing Muthesius he noted that Stüler, whom he inaccurately calls a pupil of Schinkel, had »little of the genius of his master« (Hitchcock 1928, p. 38); as late as 1958, by which time the interiors of the Neues Museum were inaccessible, Hitchcock judged it's exterior sobriety as proof of »the rapid deterioration of rationalist Grecians standards, which followed within decades (of Schinkel's career) in the hands of Schinkel's ablest pupils, is to be noted in the Neues Museum.« (Hitchcock 1958, p. 61.) This was a view once again grounded in the evaluation of Georg Poensgen, who had given an equivocating evaluation of Stüler: »When then Persius died much too young, in 1845, August Stüler, another Schinkel pupil, stepped in to take his place. But he, in contrast to Persius, was never able to liberate himself from the prototypes of their common teacher and his activity was unfortunately limited to the tasteful completion of the projects he had left behind. He survived the king by a few years, and with his death (1865) an epoch in European architecture came to an end ...« (Poensgen 1930, p. 8.)

But a fascinating reversal of fortunes is to be observed in the evolution of the critic Karl Scheffler's comments on Stüler. In a 1907 article on Behrens in *Die Zukunft*, Scheffler noted that Behrens's way of working returned directly to the last great period of architecture, »to the time of Schinkel, Strack and Stüler.« (Cited in Anderson 2001, p. 116.) Again writing of Behrens, in his 1913 *Die Architektur der Großstadt* Scheffler noted that anyone who traveled to Berlin 50 years prior would speak of the great monumental buildings: Brandenburg Gate, Schauspielhaus or Museum am Lustgarten, today friends of modern »Baukunst« would look rather to Berlin's »Nutzbauten«: including Messels Warenhaus and Behrens's work for the AEG. This change of interest announced the change in interests of the time: »It isn't that Messel and Behrens possessed a completely different type of architectural talent than Gentz, Langhans, Schinkel, Stüler or Wäsemann. On the contrary, both architects and their whole ethos are in fact carriers of tradition, they belong to the most legitimate descendants of that early talent of the Berlin school of architecture.« (Scheffler 1913, p. 128/129.) But then in 1939, perhaps in reaction to the polemical adoption of Schinkel and his pupils by the Nazis, Scheffler sharply rebukes Schinkel and his pupils for allowing architecture to culminate in grandiose and ungrounded fantasies: »The architects of classical periods were always anxious to follow the examples set by the great originals of their time and of the general stylistic trends; the modern architect began to repeat historical building forms without grasping their inner necessity and gave himself only the challenge of doing it in such a way that he alone could never be original. If building commissions were lacking, his talent would remain alive at te drafting board, in the studio, or on paper. An arbitrary, ingenious and playful architecture came into being. It had already begun with Friedrich Gilly and Schinkel. City plans or metropolitan enhacements of gigantic scale were contrived along with architecture of fantasy that were pure wishful dreams.« (Scheffler, 1939, p. 110.) In that same year Speer unveiled for Hitler's 50th birthday on 20 April 1939 the model of the great triumphal arch, the so-called Bauwerk T. That monumental project slated one of Stüler's numerous church designs for demolition, the St. Matthäuskirche in the Tiergarten district, which stood squarely in the way of the great axis planned by Speer. No one arose in it's favor, although in 1943 one of Stüler's descendants wrote a celebration of Stüler in the Nazi's luxurious art magazine *Kunst im Deutschen Reich*. (Müller-Stüler 1943.)

Although St. Matthäus's parish house was taken down already in 1939, the church remained standing as the war effort delayed further progress of Speer and Hitler's building plans. Burned to a shell in the final days of the war, the church was rebuilt – on the cultivated mistaken impression that it was a Schinkel building, according to Eva Börsch-Supan (Börsch-Supan 1997, p. 532) – by the architects Jürgen Emmerich and H. Patek between 1956 and 1960. With the construction but a few year's later of Mies van der Rohe's Neue Nationalgalerie, a first component of a planned Kulturforum that would transfer the dense Tiergarten quarter at Berlin's center into a modernist landscape of monuments on the periphery of West Berlin, Stüler's rebuilt church become one of the iconic images of a Berlin reemerging from the ashes. Mies himself chose the site, and although his temple atop a podium has long been celebrated as a piece of autonomous architecture, Mies went to great plans to align the gridded geometries of his new temple with the primary axes of the newly rebuilt 19th-century church, one of the most severely abstract of Stüler's church designs. From the museum's completion in the late 1960s one of the most famous photographic views juxtaposes the glazed wall and free-standing double T-beam steel column of Mies's building with survival of the 19th-century texture of Berlin embodied in Stüler's newly rebuilt church. Although this famous photograph appeared on the cover of the issue of *Bauwelt* celebrating the completion of Mies's first and only postwar building in Berlin in 1968, the name of Stüler once again took backstage to that of Schinkel. Echoing Mies's own assertion in 1961 that one could learn everything there was to know about architecture from the study of Schinkel's Altes Museum, Ulrich Conrads concluded his review, in which he acknowledged the reference point to the central axis of Stüler's church with the comment:

»I know of no building that is calmer, more clarified, more buoyant, as this one. It is Mies van der Rohe's most decisive step arm in arm with Schinkel.« (Conrads 1968, p. 1210.) *Bauwelt*'s editors juxtaposed their full analysis of the building with a quote from Schinkel's late publication of Orianda, to substantiate the fact that Mies's aesthetic and daring had been prepared by Schinkel's work which transcended historicism, in a way few were willing to grant Stüler: »The middle of the royal court is filled by a substructure above the platform of which there rises a great temple form nearly transparent through its use of huge sheets of plate glass. This temple, as the crowning of the entire structure, in order to break up te simple lines of Greek architecture by picturesque means, remains completely essential.« (*Bauwelt*, 16 September 1968, p. 3.)

While Stüler's buildings have stood at the very crossroads of recent German history, from the tower of St. Matthäus at the heart of the Kulturforum to the centrality of the Neues Museum to projects for the development of the Museumsinsel as both a UNESCO world-heritage site and a centerpiece of reunified Berlin's cultural politics, his name has never been coded in the ideologically charged ways that both Schinkel and Persius have by architectural modernism. Ironically enough since his entire career was devoted to pushing further the very questions that Schinkel had posed about the possibilities of architecture to go beyond historical reference to engage with the trajectories of historical development, in his *Rundbogenstil* buildings, as well as with Schinkel's insistence that new forms would develop from the attention to the possibilities of iron and new materials – such as terra cotta – as integral parts of an evolving architectural language.

Karl Friedrich Schinkel

1. Berlin-Charlottenburg, Gierkeplatz, Luisenkirche, 1823–26. Ansicht von Südwesten. 20. Juli 1998.
2. Berlin-Charlottenburg, Schloß Charlottenburg, Schlafzimmer der Königin Luise, 1810. 10. Mai 1999.

1. Berlin-Charlottenburg, Gierkeplatz, Luisenkirche, 1823–26. View from the south-west. 20 July 1998.
2. Berlin-Charlottenburg, Schloss Charlottenburg, bedroom of Queen Luise, 1810. 10 May 1999.

3. Berlin-Charlottenburg, Park des Schlosses Charlottenburg, Mausoleum, 1810–12. Ansicht von Süden. 18. Juni
1998.
4. Berlin-Charlottenburg, Park des Schlosses Charlottenburg, Mausoleum, 1810–12. Innenansicht. 1. Sept. 1998.

3. Berlin-Charlottenburg, park of Schloss Charlottenburg,
Mausoleum, 1810–12. View from the south.
18 June 1998.
4. Berlin-Charlottenburg, park of Schloss Charlottenburg,
Mausoleum, 1810–12. Interior view. 1 Sept. 1998.

5. Berlin-Charlottenburg, Park des Schlosses Charlottenburg, Neuer Pavillon, 1824/25. Ansicht von Südwesten.
18. Juni 1998.
6. Berlin-Charlottenburg, Park des Schlosses Charlottenburg, Neuer Pavillon, 1824/25. Gartensaal. 13. Juni
1999.

S. 24, 25
7. Berlin-Kreuzberg, Viktoriapark, Kreuzbergdenkmal,
1818–21. Ansicht von Süden. 24. März 2000.
8. Berlin-Kreuzberg, Kreuzbergdenkmal, 1818–21. Fialen. 24. März 2000.

5. Berlin-Charlottenburg, park of Schloss Charlottenburg, Neuer Pavillon, 1824/25. View from the south-
west. 18 June 1998.
6. Berlin-Charlottenburg, park of Schloss Charlottenburg, Neuer Pavillon, 1824/25. Garden room. 13 June
1999.

pp. 24, 25
7. Berlin-Kreuzberg, Viktoriapark, Kreuzbergdenkmal,
1818–21. View from the south. 24 March 2000.
8. Berlin-Kreuzberg, Kreuzbergdenkmal, 1818–21. Pinnacles. 24 March 2000.

9. Berlin-Mitte, Schauspielhaus, 1818–21. Giebel von Südosten. 27. April 1998.
10. Berlin-Mitte, Schauspielhaus, 1818–21. Ansicht von Nordosten. 27. April 1998.
11. Berlin-Mitte, Gendarmenmarkt, Schauspielhaus, 1818–21. Ansicht von Osten. 27. April 1998.

9. Berlin-Mitte, Schauspielhaus, 1818–21. Gable from the south-east. 27 April 1998.
10. Berlin-Mitte, Schauspielhaus, 1818–21. View from the north-east. 27 April 1998.
11. Berlin-Mitte, Gendarmenmarkt, Schauspielhaus, 1818–21. View from the east. 27 April 1998.

S. 28, 29
12. Berlin-Mitte, Altes Museum, 1823–29. Südöstlicher Teil der Säulenvorhalle mit Löwenkämpfer und kämpfender Amazone. 24. April 1998
13. Berlin-Mitte, Altes Museum, 1823–29. Südwestlicher Teil der Säulenvorhalle von innen. 18. Okt. 1999.

pp. 28, 29
12. Berlin-Mitte, Altes Museum, 1823–29. South-eastern part of the colonnade with lion fighter and fighting Amazon. 24 April 1998.
13. Berlin-Mitte, Altes Museum, 1823–29. Interior view of the south-western part of the colonnade. 18 Okt. 1999.

14. Berlin-Mitte, Altes Museum, 1823–29. Treppenhaus. 22. Feb. 2000.
15. Berlin-Mitte, Altes Museum, 1823–29. Rotunde.
3. Sept. 1998.

14. Berlin-Mitte, Altes Museum, 1823–29. Staircase.
22 Feb. 2000.
15. Berlin-Mitte, Altes Museum, 1823–29. Rotunda.
3 Sept. 1998.

32

16. Berlin-Mitte, Altes Museum, 1823–29. Kuppel der Rotunde. 17. Aug. 1998.
17. Berlin-Mitte, Altes Museum, Granitschale im Lustgarten, 1827–34. 18. Okt. 1999.

16. Berlin-Mitte, Altes Museum, 1823–29. Dome of the rotunda. 17 Aug. 1998.
17. Berlin-Mitte, Altes Museum, granite shell in the Lustgarten, 1827–34. 18 Oct. 1999.

21. Berlin-Mitte, Unter den Linden, Schloßbrücke, 1821
bis 1824. Ansicht vom Lustgarten Richtung Friedrichswerdersche Kirche. 18. Okt. 1999.
22. Berlin-Mitte, Unter den Linden, Schloßbrücke, 1821
bis 1824. Brüstungsplatte, Tritonen. 18. Okt. 1999.
23. Berlin-Mitte, Unter den Linden, Schloßbrücke, 1821
bis 1824. Brüstungsplatten, Seepferde. 18. Okt. 1999.

21. Berlin-Mitte, Unter den Linden, Schloßbrücke, 1821
to 1824. View from the Lustgarten towards the Friedrichswerdersche Kirche. 18 Okt. 1999.
22. Berlin-Mitte, Unter den Linden, Schloßbrücke, 1821
to 1824. Parapet slab, tritons. 18 Oct. 1999.
23. Berlin-Mitte, Unter den Linden, Schloßbrücke,1821
to 1824. Parapet slab, seahorses. 18 Oct. 1999.

24. Berlin-Mitte, Friedrichswerdersche Kirche, 1824–30. Innenansicht zum Chor. 5. Mai 1999.
25. Berlin-Mitte, Werderstraße, Friedrichswerdersche Kirche, 1824–30. Ansicht von Südwesten. 18. Okt. 1999.

24. Berlin-Mitte, Friedrichswerdersche Kirche, 1824–30. Interior view towards the choir. 5 May 1999.
25. Berlin-Mitte, Werderstraße, Friedrichswerdersche Kirche, 1824–30. View from the south-west. 18 Oct. 1999.

26. Berlin-Reinickendorf (Tegel), Humboldtschlösschen, 1820–24. Gartenseite von Westen. 7. Juni 1999.
27. Berlin-Reinickendorf (Tegel), Karolinenstraße, Humboldtschlösschen, 1820–24. Eingangsseite von Nordosten. 17. Juli 1998.
28. Berlin-Reinickendorf (Tegel), Humboldtschlösschen, 1820–24. Vestibül. 7. Juni 1999.

26. Berlin-Reinickendorf (Tegel), Humboldtschlösschen, 1820–24. Garden side from the west. 7 June 1999.
27. Berlin-Reinickendorf (Tegel), Karolinenstraße, Humboldtschlösschen, 1820–24. Entrance side from the north-east. 17 July 1998.
28. Berlin-Reinickendorf (Tegel), Humboldtschlösschen, 1820–24. Vestibule. 7 June 1999.

29. Berlin-Reinickendorf (Tegel), Park des Humboldt-schlösschens, Grabstätte mit »Spes« von Bertel Thor-valdsen und Exedra. 1829. 7. Juni 1999.
30. Berlin-Wedding, Kirche St. Paul, 1832–34. Südost-seite (Pankstraße). 25. März 1998.

29. Berlin-Reinickendorf (Tegel), park of the Humboldt-schlösschen, burial place with »Spes« by Bertel Thor-valdsen and exedra. 1829. 7 June 1999.
30. Berlin-Wedding, church of St. Paul, 1832–34. South-east side (Pankstraße). 25 March 1998.

31. Berlin-Wedding, Nazarethkirche, 1832–34. West-seite. 25. März 1998.
32. Berlin-Wedding, Leopoldplatz, Nazarethkirche, 1832–34. Südseite. 25. März 1998.

S. 46, 47
33. Berlin-Zehlendorf (Wannsee), Glienicke, Große Neugierde, 1835. 7. April 1999.
34. Berlin-Zehlendorf (Wannsee), Glienicke, Kleine Neugierde, 1825. 7. April 1999.

31. Berlin-Wedding, Nazarethkirche, 1832–34. West side. 25 March 1998.
32. Berlin-Wedding, Leopoldplatz, Nazarethkirche, 1832–34. South side. 25 March 1998.

pp. 46, 47
33. Berlin-Zehlendorf (Wannsee), Glienicke, Große Neugierde, 1835. 7 April 1999.
34. Berlin-Zehlendorf (Wannsee), Glienicke, Kleine Neugierde, 1825. 7 April 1999.

35. Berlin-Zehlendorf (Wannsee), Glienicke, Schloß, 1825–28. 25. Aug. 1998.
36. Berlin-Zehlendorf (Wannsee), Glienicke, Kasino, 1824/25. Kopf der nordöstlichen Pergola. 27. Aug. 1999.
37. Berlin-Zehlendorf (Wannsee), Glienicke, Kasino, 1824/25. Ansicht mit südwestlicher Pergola. 7. April 1999.

35. Berlin-Zehlendorf (Wannsee), Glienicke, Schloss, 1825–28. 25 Aug. 1998.
36. Berlin-Zehlendorf (Wannsee), Glienicke, Kasino, 1824/25. End of the north-eastern pergola. 27 Aug. 1999.
37. Berlin-Zehlendorf (Wannsee), Glienicke, Kasino, 1824/25. View with south-western pergola. 7 April 1999..

38. Berlin-Zehlendorf (Wannsee), Pfaueninsel, Schweizerhaus, 1829/30. Westseite. 20. Juli 1998.
39. Berlin-Zehlendorf (Wannsee), Pfaueninsel, Kavalierhaus, 1824–26. 20. Juli 1998.
40. Potsdam, Pfingstberg, Pomona-Tempel, 1800/01. 4. Aug. 1998.

38. Berlin-Zehlendorf (Wannsee), Pfaueninsel, Schweizerhaus, 1829/30. West side. 20 July 1998.
39. Berlin-Zehlendorf (Wannsee), Pfaueninsel, Kavalierhaus, 1824–26. 20 July 1998.
40. Potsdam, Pfingstberg, Pomona-Tempel, 1800/01. 4 Aug. 1998.

S. 52, 53
41. Potsdam, Alter Markt, Nikolaikirche, 1830–37. Ansicht von Südosten. 24. Juli 1998.
42. Potsdam, Alter Markt, Nikolaikirche, 1830–37. Innenansicht. 24. Juli 1998.

pp. 52, 53
41. Potsdam, Alter Markt, Nikolaikirche, 1830–37. View from the south-east. 24 July 1998.
42. Potsdam, Alter Markt, Nikolaikirche, 1830–37. Interior view. 24 July 1998.

43. Potsdam, Sanssouci, Schloß Charlottenhof,
1826–29. Ansicht von Nordosten. 11. Aug. 1998.
44. Potsdam, Sanssouci, Schloß Charlottenhof,
1826–29. Gartenfassade. 11. Aug. 1998.
45. Potsdam, Sanssouci, Schloß Charlottenhof,
1826–29. Portikus auf der Westseite. 14. Sept. 1998.

43. Potsdam, Sanssouci, Schloss Charlottenhof,
1826–29. View from the north-east. 11 Aug. 1998.
44. Potsdam, Sanssouci, Schloss Charlottenhof,
1826–29. Garden façade. 11 Aug. 1998.
45. Potsdam, Sanssouci, Schloss Charlottenhof,
1826–29. Portico of the west side. 14 Sept. 1998.

46. Potsdam, Sanssouci, Schloß Charlottenhof,
1826–29. Vestibül. 14. Sept. 1998.
47. Potsdam, Sanssouci, Schloß Charlottenhof,
1826–29. Zeltzimmer. 14. Sept. 1998.
48. Potsdam, Sanssouci, Schloß Charlottenhof,
1826–29. Gartensaal. 14. Sept. 1998.

46. Potsdam, Sanssouci, Schloss Charlottenhof,
1826–29. Vestibule. 14 Sept. 1998.
47. Potsdam, Sanssouci, Schloss Charlottenhof,
1826–29. Tented room. 14 Sept. 1998.
48. Potsdam, Sanssouci, Schloss Charlottenhof,
1826–29. Garden room. 14 Sept. 1998.

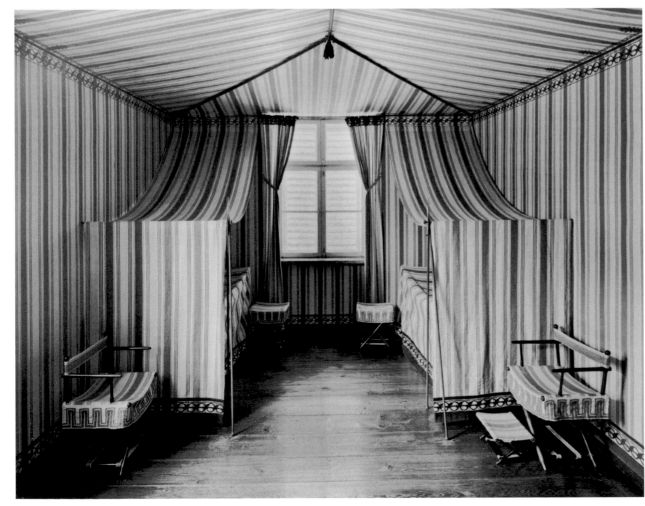

49. Potsdam, Sanssouci, Römische Bäder, 1829–39.
Ansicht von Süden. 11. Aug. 1998.
50. Potsdam, Sanssouci, Römische Bäder, 1829–39.
Ansicht von Südosten. 14. Sept. 1998.
51. Potsdam, Sanssouci, Römische Bäder, 1829–39.
Große Laube. 14. Sept.1998.

49. Potsdam, Sanssouci, Römische Bäder, 1829–39.
View from the south. 11 Aug. 1998.
50. Potsdam, Sanssouci, Römische Bäder, 1829–39.
View from the south-east. 14 Sept. 1998.
51. Potsdam, Sanssouci, Römische Bäder, 1829–39.
Große Laube. 14 Sept.1998.

52. Potsdam, Sanssouci, Römische Bäder, 1829–39.
Thermen. 5. Juni 1999.
53. Potsdam, Sanssouci, Römische Bäder, 1829–39.
Impluvium. 14. Sept. 1998.

52. Potsdam, Sanssouci, Römische Bäder, 1829–39.
Thermal springs. 5 June 1999.
53. Potsdam, Sanssouci, Römische Bäder, 1829–39.
Impluvium. 14 Sept. 1998.

Ludwig Persius

1. Berlin-Zehlendorf, Park Glienicke, Jägertor, 1842/43.
Ansicht von Norden. 20. Aug. 2002.
2. Berlin-Zehlendorf, Park Glienicke, Jägertor, 1842/43.
Detailansicht. 20. Aug. 2002.

1. Berlin-Zehlendorf, Park Glienicke, Jägertor, 1842/43.
View from the north. 20 Aug. 2002.
2. Berlin-Zehlendorf, Park Glienicke, Jägertor, 1842/43.
Detailed view. 20 Aug. 2002.

3. Berlin-Zehlendorf, Park Glienicke, Maschinen- und Gärtnerhaus, 1838. Ansicht von Süden. 22. Aug. 2002.
4. Berlin-Zehlendorf, Schloß Glienicke, Wirtschaftshof, 1845. Ehemaliger Pferde- und Kuhstall. 9. Aug. 2002.

3. Berlin-Zehlendorf, Park Glienicke, power and gardener's house, 1838. View from the south. 22 Aug. 2002.
4. Berlin-Zehlendorf, Schloss Glienicke, farmyard, 1845. Former stable for horses and cows. 9 Aug. 2002.

23. Potsdam, Park Sanssouci, Fasanerie, 1842–44.
Ansicht von Norden. 17. Aug. 2002.
24. Potsdam, Park Sanssouci, Fasanerie, 1842–44.
Ansicht von Nordwesten. 17. Aug. 2002.
25. Potsdam, Park Sanssouci, Fasanerie, 1842–44.
Ansicht von Südwesten. 10. Aug. 2002.

23. Potsdam, Park Sanssouci, Fasanerie, 1842–44.
View from the north. 17 Aug. 2002.
24. Potsdam, Park Sanssouci, Fasanerie, 1842–44.
View from the north-west. 17 Aug. 2002.
25. Potsdam, Park Sanssouci, Fasanerie, 1842–44.
View from the south-west. 10 Aug. 2002.

26. Potsdam, Park Sanssouci, Hofgärtnerhaus, 1829–32.
Ansicht von Westen. 9. Dez. 2002.
27. Potsdam, Park Sanssouci, Hofgärtnerhaus, 1829–32.
Ansicht von Osten. 9. Dez. 2002.

S. 90, 91
28. Potsdam, Park Sanssouci, Ruinenberg, Normannischer Turm, 1845/46. Turm und Zirkusmauer.
29. Aug. 2002.
29. Potsdam, Park Sanssouci, Ruinenberg, Exedra,
1843/44. Blick auf Krongut Bornstedt. 29. Aug. 2002.

26. Potsdam, Park Sanssouci, Hofgärtnerhaus, 1829–32.
View from the west. 9 Dec. 2002.
27. Potsdam, Park Sanssouci, Hofgärtnerhaus, 1829–32.
View from the east. 9 Dec. 2002.

pp. 90, 91
28. Potsdam, Park Sanssouci, Ruinenberg, Normannischer Turm, 1845/46. Tower and circus wall.
29 Aug. 2002.
29. Potsdam, Park Sanssouci, Ruinenberg, exedra,
1843/44. View of Krongut Bornstedt. 29 Aug. 2002.

34. Sacrow, Krampitzer Straße, Heilandskirche, 1843/44. Ansicht von Westen. 29. Okt. 2002.

35. Sacrow, Krampitzer Straße, Heilandskirche, 1843/44. Ansicht von Südwesten. 29. Okt. 2002.

34. Sacrow, Krampitzer Straße, Heilandskirche, 1843/44. View from the west. 29 Oct. 2002.

35. Sacrow, Krampitzer Straße, Heilandskirche, 1843/44. View from the south-west. 29 Oct. 2002.

Friedrich August Stüler

1. Berlin-Charlottenburg, Spandauer Damm, Ecke Schloßstraße, ehemalige Garde-du-Corps-Kasernen, 1851–59. Westlicher Stülerbau von Norden. 21. Juli 2003.
2. Berlin-Charlottenburg, Spandauer Damm Ecke Schloßstraße, ehemalige Garde-du-Corps-Kasernen, 1851–59. Kuppel des westlichen Stülerbaus. 21. Juli 2003.

1. Berlin-Charlottenburg, Spandauer Damm / Schloßstraße junction, former Garde-du-Corps-Kasernen, 1851–59. Western Stüler building from the north. 21 July 2003.
2. Berlin-Charlottenburg, Spandauer Damm / Schloßstraße junction, former Garde-du-Corps-Kasernen, 1851–59. Cupola of the western Stüler building. 21 July 2003.

3. Berlin-Marzahn, Alt Marzahn, ev. Dorfkirche, 1870/71.
Ansicht von Südosten. 17. März 2004.
4. Berlin-Marzahn, Alt Marzahn, ev. Dorfkirche, 1870/71.
Blick zum Altar. 17. März 2004.
5. Berlin-Marzahn, Alt Marzahn, ev. Dorfkirche, 1870/71.
Blick zur Orgel. 17. März 2004.

3. Berlin-Marzahn, Alt Marzahn, Prot. village church,
1870/71. View from the south-west. 17 March 2004.
4. Berlin-Marzahn, Alt Marzahn, Prot. village church,
1870/71. View towards the altar. 17 March 2004.
5. Berlin-Marzahn, Alt Marzahn, Prot. village church,
1870/71. View towards the organ. 17 March 2004.

6. Berlin-Mitte, Bodestraße 3, Alte Nationalgalerie, 1867–76. Rückseite mit Exedra. 26. April 2004.
7. Berlin-Mitte, Bodestraße 3, Alte Nationalgalerie, 1867–76. Südwestfassade und Treppenanlage. 18. März 2002.

S. 106, 107
8. Berlin-Mitte, Bodestraße 4, Neues Museum, 1843 bis 1846, 1855, 1865. Mittelrisalit von Nordosten. 15. Nov. 2004.
9. Berlin-Mitte, Bodestraße 4, Neues Museum, 1843 bis 1846, 1855, 1865. Römischer Saal. 8. Mai 2003.

6. Berlin-Mitte, Bodestraße 3, Alte Nationalgalerie, 1867–76. Backside with exedra. 26 April 2004.
7. Berlin-Mitte, Bodestraße 3, Alte Nationalgalerie, 1867–76. South-west façade and stairs. 18 March 2002.

pp. 106, 107
8. Berlin-Mitte, Bodestraße 4, Neues Museum, 1843 to 1846, 1855, 1865. Central prodruding section from the north-east. 15 Nov. 2004.
9. Berlin-Mitte, Bodestraße 4, Neues Museum, 1843 to 1846, 1855, 1865. Roman hall. 8 May 2003.

10. Berlin-Pankow, Breite Straße, Prot. village church, 1857–59. Westlicher Anbau. 15. März 2004.
11. Berlin-Pankow, Breite Straße, ev. Dorfkirche, 1857 bis 1859. Mittelalterlicher Teil, Ansicht von Nordosten. 15. März 2004.

10. Berlin-Pankow, Breite Straße, Prot. village church, 1857–59. Western extension. 15 March 2004.
11. Berlin-Pankow, Breite Straße, Prot. village church, 1857–59. Medieval part, view from the north-east. 15 March 2004.

12. Berlin-Tiergarten, Alt Moabit 25, ev. Kirche St. Johannis, 1851–57. Arkadenhalle. 17. März 2004.
13. Berlin-Tiergarten, Alt Moabit 25, ev. Kirche St. Johannis, 1851–57. Arkadenhalle. 17. März 2004.

12. Berlin-Tiergarten, Alt Moabit 25, Prot. church of St. Johannis, 1851–57. Arcaded hall. 17 March 2004.
13. Berlin-Tiergarten, Alt Moabit 25, Prot. church of St. Johannis, 1851–57. Arcaded hall. 17 March 2004.

14. Berlin-Tiergarten, Matthäikirchplatz, ev. Kirche St. Matthäus, 1844–46. Ansicht von der Neuen Nationalgalerie. 21. Mai 2003.
15. Berlin-Tiergarten, Matthäikirchplatz, ev. Kirche St. Matthäus, 1844–46. Die Apsiden von Südwesten. 21. Mai 2003.

14. Berlin-Tiergarten, Matthäikirchplatz, Prot. church of St. Matthäus, 1844–46. View from the Neue Nationalgalerie. 21 May 2003.
15. Berlin-Tiergarten, Matthäikirchplatz, Prot. church of St. Matthäus, 1844–46. The apses from the south-west. 21 May 2003.

S. 114, 115
16. Berlin-Zehlendorf (Wannsee), ev. Kirche St. Peter und Paul auf Nikolskoe, 1834–37. Ansicht von Nordosten. 28. März 2003.
17. Berlin-Zehlendorf (Wannsee), ev. Kirche St. Peter und Paul auf Nikolskoe, 1834–37. Ansicht von Südosten. 28. März 2003.

pp. 114, 115
16. Berlin-Zehlendorf (Wannsee), Prot. church of St. Peter und Paul auf Nikolskoe, 1834–37. View from the north-east. 28 March 2003.
17. Berlin-Zehlendorf (Wannsee), Prot. church of St. Peter und Paul auf Nikolskoe, 1834–37. View from the south-east. 28 March 2003.

18. Berlin-Zehlendorf (Wannsee), Wilhelmplatz, ev. Dorfkirche, 1858/59. Ansicht von Süden. 14. März 2003.
19. Berlin-Zehlendorf (Wannsee), Wilhelmplatz, ev. Dorfkirche, 1858/59. Portal und Radfenster. 14. März 2003.

18. Berlin-Zehlendorf (Wannsee), Wilhelmplatz, Prot.
village church, 1858/59. View from the south. 14 March
2003.
19. Berlin-Zehlendorf (Wannsee), Wilhelmplatz, Prot.
village church, 1858 to 1859. Portal and wheel window.
14 March 2003.

20. Caputh, Straße der Einheit, ev. Kirche, 1850–52.
Ansicht von Nordwesten. 12. März 2003.
21. Caputh, Straße der Einheit, ev. Kirche, 1850–52.
Blick zur Orgel.12. März 2003.
22. Caputh, Marienquelle, 1855. 26. April 2004.

20. Caputh, Straße der Einheit, Prot. church, 1850–52.
View from the north-west. 12 March 2003.
21. Caputh, Straße der Einheit, Prot. church, 1850 to
1852. View towards the organ. 12 March 2003.
22. Caputh, Marienquelle, 1855. 26 April 2004.

23. Potsdam, Park Sanssouci, Orangerieschloß, 1850 bis 1860. Ansicht von Süden. 14. Juni 2004.
24. Potsdam, Park Sanssouci, Orangerieschloß, 1850 bis 1860. Blick zum Belvedere. 14. Juni 2004.

S. 122, 123
25. Potsdam, Ribbeckstraße, ev. Kirche, 1855/56. Turm und Arkaden. 24. Juli 2003.
26. Potsdam, Ribbeckstraße, ev. Kirche, 1855/56. Arkaden. 24. Juli 2003.

23. Potsdam, Park Sanssouci, Orangerieschloß, 1850 to 1860. View from the south. 14 June 2004.
24. Potsdam, Park Sanssouci, Orangerieschloß, 1850 to 1860. View towards the belvedere. 14 June 2004.

pp. 122, 123
25. Potsdam, Ribbeckstraße, Prot. church, 1855/56. Tower and arcades. 24 July 2003.
26. Potsdam, Ribbeckstraße, Prot. church, 1855/56. Arcades. 24 July 2003.

27. Potsdam, Ribbeckstraße, ev. Kirche, 1855/56.
Ansicht von Südwesten. 24. Juli 2003.
28. Potsdam, Schopenhauerstraße, Weinbergstor,
1850/51. Ansicht von Süden. 28. April 2004.

27. Potsdam, Ribbeckstraße, Prot. church, 1855/56.
View from the south-west. 24 July 2003.
28. Potsdam, Schopenhauerstraße, Weinbergstor,
1850/51. View from the south. 28 April 2004.

Katalog Karl Friedrich Schinkel

MAB   Martina Abri
HIB   Hillert Ibbeken
HSCH Heinz Schönemann

1. Berlin Charlottenburg, Gierkeplatz, Luisen-kirche, 1823–26

Die Kirche wurde 1823–26 von Schinkel erneuert, der das Innere umgestaltete und einen Turm anfügte. Sie brannte 1943 aus, bei der Renovierung von 1950–56 wurden die Schinkelschen Konstruktionen des Inneren nicht wiederhergestellt, damit ist heute nur noch der Turm von Schinkel. Er ist dreigeschossig, Fenster und Schmuckbänder sind in allen Geschossen gleich gehalten. Der Name Luisenkirche bezieht sich auf Königin Luise, die im Volk ungemein beliebt war. HIB

2. Berlin-Charlottenburg, Schloß Charlottenburg, Schlafzimmer der Königin Luise, 1810

Königin Luise kehrte im Dezember 1809 mit dem König aus dem Exil in Memel nach Berlin zurück, starb aber schon im Juli 1810. In diese kurze Zeitspanne fällt der Entwurf des wohl berühmtesten Möbelstücks von Schinkel, des Schiffbetts der Königin, des »lit bateau«, eine seiner ersten Schöpfungen für das Königshaus. Die Schmalseiten enden in den Voluten ionischer Kapitelle, sie sind ganz gleich, so daß Kopf- und Fußende nicht als solche angesprochen werden können, sie tragen je eine Polsterrolle. Die lange Seite des aus hellem Birkenholz gefertigten Bettes wird von einer geschwungenen Girlande gerahmt, die in flatternden Bändern endet. Die beiden Blumentischchen bargen früher vielleicht gläserne oder silberne Waschgeschirre. Die Wände werden von herabfallenden, gerafften Falten von weißem Mousseline strukturiert, einem fast durchsichtigen Baumwollstoff, durch den das Rosarot der Tapete als Symbol der Morgenröte schimmert. HIB

3, 4. Berlin-Charlottenburg, Park des Schlosses Charlottenburg, Mausoleum, 1810–12

Gleich nach dem Tode der Königin Luise im Juli 1810 entwarf der König eine Skizze des Mausoleums, in dem er seine Gemahlin zu begraben wünschte. Schinkel setzte die Zeichnung um und baute einen viersäuligen Portikus aus Sandstein, der 1828 durch roten Granit ersetzt wurde, das »vaterländische« Gestein. Der Sandstein-Portikus wurde auf der Pfaueninsel wieder errichtet. Heinrich Gentz gestaltete das Innere des Mausoleums. Hier stand, zunächst allein, der Marmorsarkophag der Königin, 1811–14 von Christian Daniel Rauch geschaffen. Die Königin ist als Schlafende dargestellt, mit faltenreichem Gewand. Der Sockel mit Wappen und Adler geht auf Schinkel zurück, ebenso wie die beiden großen Kandelaber. Der eine stammt von Friedrich Tieck, der andere ebenfalls von Rauch. 1840, mit dem Tode von Friedrich Wilhelm III., wurde das Mausoleum vergrößert, 1846 wurde der Marmorsarkophag des Königs aufgestellt. HIB

5, 6. Berlin-Charlottenburg, Park des Schlosses Charlottenburg, Neuer Pavillon, 1824/25

In der Südostecke des Parks, am Kopf des hinter dem Schloß entlangführenden Weges, liegt das auch Schinkelpavillon genannte Gebäude, das Friedrich Wilhelm III. 1824/25 erbauen ließ, um es mit seiner zwei-ten, in morganatischer Ehe angetrauten Gemahlin zu bewohnen. Das Haus ist eine Nachschöpfung der nicht mehr existierenden königlichen Casina del Chiatamone bei Neapel, wo der König 1822 residiert hatte. Der fast kubische Bau wird im ersten Stock vollständig von einem zarten Balkon umrahmt, jede der vier Seiten lockern große Loggien auf, die eine deutliche Verbindung von Innen und Außen schaffen, wie etwa beim Alten Museum (Abb. 13), dem Schweizerhaus auf der Pfaueninsel (Abb. 38) oder dem Gesellschaftshaus in Magdeburg. Vom Park kommend, wird der Blick von zwei Granitsäulen mit bronzenen Viktorien von Christian Daniel Rauch flankiert, die 1840 aufgestellt wurden. Kübel mit Palmen betonen das südliche Gepräge. Wichtigster Raum im Inneren ist der Gartensaal mit einer großen, halbrunden Wandnische, die Schinkel der Rundbank der Priesterin Mammia an der pompejanischen Gräberstraße nachbildete. In das Halbrund ist ein Wandbehang mit weitem Faltenwurf gespannt, ein blauer Stoff mit goldenen Borten und Sternen. In der Mitte steht, erhöht, eine weibliche Marmorfigur, die eine Schale trägt. Der Neue Pavillon brannte 1943 aus, er wurde in den Jahren 1957–70 vollständig wiederhergestellt. HIB

7, 8. Berlin-Kreuzberg, Viktoriapark, Kreuzberg-denkmal, 1818–21

Wie bei der Friedrichswerderschen Kirche und der Neuen Wache gab es auch beim Kreuzbergdenkmal viele von der endgültigen Form ganz abweichende Vorentwürfe. Den Zuschlag erhielt ein obeliskartiger Turm, der an gotische Turmhelme erinnert, mit zahlreichen Fialen und einem eisernen Kreuz an der Spitze. Das Kreuzbergdenkmal ist ein Nationaldenkmal zur Erinnerung an die Siege der Befreiungskriege. Über kreuzförmigem Grundriß erhebt sich das knapp 20 Meter hohe, dunkelgrün lackierte Denkmal, umlaufend sind 12 Nischen eingetieft, die 12 Schlachten gewidmet sind. In den Nischen stehen 12 Genien, die von Christian Daniel Rauch, Friedrich Tieck und Ludwig Wichmann modelliert wurden. Mit ihren Köpfen werden Mitglieder des Königshauses und Heerführer porträtiert, darunter auch Zar Alexander I. von Russland. Das Denkmal wurde 1878 um 8 Meter angehoben und auf einen Sockel von Johann Heinrich Strack gestellt, um weithin sichtbar zu bleiben. Eine Restaurierung 1980–83 brachte nicht den gewünschten Erfolg, so daß 1996 eine weitere, aufwendige Restaurierung notwendig wurde, die, im September 2000 abgeschlossen, einschließlich des Sockels 7 Millionen Mark verschlang. Das Denkmal selbst, ein Werk der Berliner Königlichen Eisengießerei, dessen Gußqualität von heutigen Spezialisten gerühmt wird, hatte seinerzeit 78 365 Taler gekostet. HIB

9–11. Berlin-Mitte, Gendarmenmarkt, Schauspiel-haus, 1818–21

Nachdem das von dem älteren Langhans gebaute Theater am 29. Juli 1817 während einer Probe zu Schillers Räubern Feuer gefangen hatte und abgebrannt war, beauftragte Friedrich Wilhelm III. Schinkel am 30. April 1818 mit der Ausführung eines Neubaus, der soweit wie möglich die alten Grundmauern wieder verwenden sollte. In den Jahren 1818–21 baute Schinkel eine dreiteilige Anlage, die ein Theater, einen Konzertsaal sowie Magazin- und Probenräume umfasste. Die Achse des Mittelteiles ist quer zur Achse des Gendarmenmarktes gestellt, während ihr die beiden Seitenteile folgen. Der Bau ist fast vollständig durchfenstert, es gibt keine Rundbögen. Die beiden Obergeschosse sind von Pilastern gegliedert, das Untergeschoß für die Magazinräume und die Heizung bildet einen hohen Sockel, den vor dem Mittelteil eine steile Freitreppe überspannt. Über dieser Freitreppe erhebt sich ein Portikus mit ionischer Säulenhalle und reich geschmücktem Giebel. Er erzählt die Geschichte der Niobiden als Sinnbild der Tragödie. Der Giebel wiederholt sich an der Front des höher ragenden Bühnenhauses, hier steht der nackte, geflügelte Eros vor einem Thron. Diesen Giebel krönt Apoll auf einem Greifengespann. Auf den Dachecken stehen die neun Musen. Das Schauspielhaus brannte am Kriegsende vollständig aus, von der aufwendigen Inneneinrichtung ist so gut wie nichts erhalten. Der Wiederaufbau wurde 1984 abgeschlossen, das Haus dient heute nur noch als Konzerthaus. HIB

12–16. Berlin-Mitte, Lustgarten, Altes Museum, 1823–29

Nach den Siegen über Napoleon kehrten die geraubten Kunstschätze nach Berlin zurück, allein es fehlten geeignete Ausstellungsräume, auch für weitere königliche Sammlungen. Schinkel entwickelte 1822 einen Plan für einen neuen Museumsbau am Lustgarten, gegenüber dem königlichen Schloß, der von Friedrich Wilhelm III. mit der Auflage genehmigt wurde, die Kosten von 700 000 Talern nicht zu überschreiten. 1823 wurde mit dem Bau begonnen, der bis 1829 dauerte, 1830 war die Einweihung. Dem imposanten Bauplatz in der Mitte der Stadt entspricht eine imposante Architektur mit einer breiten ionischen Säulenhalle, die sich zum Lustgarten und letztlich zum heute nicht mehr vorhandenen Schloß hin öffnet. Die vierflügelige Anlage gruppiert sich um einen zentralen Mittelteil, der das Gebäude überragt und einen großen, durch beide Geschosse gehenden Kuppelsaal enthält: die dem Pantheon in Rom nachempfundene Rotunde. Zu dem Gebäude führt eine breite, vorgelagerte Treppe, über die man in ein offenes Treppenhaus gelangt, das das Innere und Äußere des Museums auf das glücklichste miteinander verbindet. Dem steht heute leider eine zwischen die inneren Säulen gehängte Glaswand entgegen, die jedoch wieder abgebaut werden soll. Das Museum brannte im Kriege aus und wurde bis 1966 äußerlich wiederhergerichtet. Es enthält heute im Erdgeschoß die Antikensammlung und im Obergeschoß Ausstellungsräume. HIB

17. Berlin-Mitte, Altes Museum, Granitschale im Lustgarten, 1827–34

Die Schale, knapp 7 Meter im Durchmesser und etwa 1600 Zentner schwer, ist aus Granit, »aus vaterländischem Gestein«, wie man damals sagte, in der irrigen Annahme, Granit stünde auch in Brandenburg an. Die eiszeitliche Herkunft als Geschiebe aus Skandinavien war damals noch nicht akzeptiert. Der Berliner Bauinspektor Cantian hatte den riesigen Block entdeckt, aus dem die Schale geschlagen wurde, einen der Markgrafensteine in den Rauener Bergen bei Fürstenwalde, wo dessen Reste noch heute bewundert werden können. Die Schale wurde an Ort und Stelle grob zugeschlagen und mit einem eigens gebauten Kahn über die Spree nach Berlin verschifft. Dort wollte sie Schinkel in der Rotunde des Alten Museums aufstellen, nahm davon aber Abstand, weil die Schale noch größer, als ursprünglich geplant, ausgefallen war. So wurde sie vor die Freitreppe des Museums gestellt. Die Schale war in damaliger

Zeit ein Wunder der Technik und bei weitem die größte ihrer Art. HIB

18, 19. Berlin-Mitte, Oberwallstraße, Details der ehemaligen Bauakademie, 1832–36

Die Bauakademie, Schinkels moderner Zweckbau, brannte 1945 aus, die Ruine wurde 1962 beseitigt, um Platz für den Bau des DDR-Außenministeriums zu schaffen. Viele Schmuckelemente des Baus sind jedoch erhalten, darunter Teile der nebeneinander gelegenen Hauptportale, das linke führte in die Allgemeine Bauschule, das rechte in die Gewerbeschule. An der sogenannten Schinkelklause hinter dem Kronprinzenpalais wurde das Gewände des linken Tores mit dem rechten Portal vermauert. Mit einer Ausnahme setzte man die von August Kiß nach Zeichnungen von Schinkel modellierten Terrakottaplatten korrekt wieder ein. Die Platten erzählen symbolisch die Entwicklung der Baukunst. Das dritte Bild von unten links zeigt ein kniendes Mädchen mit einem Blätterkorb voller Ähren: der korinthische Stil, das Pendant auf der rechten Seite versinnbildlicht den ionischen Stil. Links oben findet sich Orpheus mit der Leier, oben rechts Amphion, der die Burg des siebentorigen Theben durch den Klang seiner Leier erbaute, eine Anspielung auf das Zusammenwirken von Architektur und Musik. Die sieben Platten des Türsturzes dazwischen zeigen aus Akanthus aufragende Genien. Die Türblätter geben Porträtköpfe von Baumeistern und Bildhauern wieder, darunter Brunelleschi, den Erbauer der Kuppel des Florentiner Domes. Das linke Portal wurde auf einer Ausstellung der Technischen Universität Berlin gezeigt, ebenfalls mit Köpfen berühmter Meister, darunter Raffael, als R. Urbino bezeichnet. Die Entscheidung für einen Wiederaufbau der Bauakademie ist noch nicht gefallen, der Bildungsverein Bautechnik errichtet zur Zeit eine Gebäudeecke als Musterfassade, die im Frühjahr 2001 fertig sein soll. HIB

20. Berlin-Mitte, Unter den Linden, Neue Wache, 1817/18

Die Neue Wache war der erste Staatsauftrag an Schinkel nach den Napoleonischen Kriegen. Nach verschiedenen Vorentwürfen entschied sich der König für den Entwurf »einem römischen Castrum ungefähr nachgebildet«. Die Neue Wache, ein Kubus auf quadratischem Grundriß, liegt im Kastanienwäldchen zwischen der Humboldt Universität und dem Zeughaus, dem heutigen Deutschen Historischen Museum. Die Straßenfront des verputzten Backsteingebäudes bildet eine tiefgestaffelte dorische Säulenvorhalle aus sächsischem Sandstein, deren Giebel 1842–46 von August Kiß nach Entwürfen von Schinkel gestaltet wurde. Nach der Novemberrevolution 1918 stand die Neue Wache leer, bis sie 1931 von Heinrich Tessenow in ein Ehrenmal für die Gefallenen des Ersten Weltkriegs umgebaut wurde. Der offene Hof wurde dabei überdacht. Seit 1993 ist die Neue Wache die Zentrale Gedenkstätte der Bundesrepublik Deutschland. HIB

21–23. Berlin-Mitte, Unter den Linden, Schloßbrücke, 1821–24

Schinkel schrieb: » Die ehemalige Hundebrücke am Zeughause war eine gewöhnliche hölzerne Jochbrücke, welche in der Umgebung von so imposanten Gebäuden, wie das Zeughaus und das königl. Schloß, ein höchst dürftiges Ansehen hatte, und diese in ihrer Art

unvergleichlich schöne Straße auf das Unschicklichste verengte und verunstaltete ...« Der König befahl den Bau einer breiten und ansehnlichen Brücke, die weder den Straßen- noch den Schiffsverkehr stören sollte. Schinkel entwarf und baute eine dreibogige, den Fluß schräg überspannende Brücke mit 4 Postamenten auf jeder Seite. Die Marmorfiguren stellen Helden und Siegesgöttinen »ganz ideal« dar: »Ein junger Held von einer Siegesgöttin in den Kampf geführt, ein Held von ihr gekrönt, ein Held im Kampf von ihr unterstützt, ein sterbender Held in ihren Armen und dergl.«. Die Brücke wird dadurch zu einem weiteren Denkmal der Befreiungskriege. Das gußeiserne Geländer mit schweren Brüstungsplatten, von der Berliner Königlichen Eisengießerei gefertigt, zeigt abwechselnd Tritonen und Seepferde, jeweils gegenständig angeordnet. HIB

24, 25. Berlin-Mitte, Werderstraße, Friedrichswerdersche Kirche, 1824–30

Als erster repräsentativer Backsteinbau besitzt die Friedrichswerdersche Kirche gerade heute eine große Bedeutung, da es der einzige öffentliche Bau Schinkels in Berlin ist, der sich in seiner Gesamtheit von Innen und Außen erhalten hat. Das Verlangen des Königs nach einer Kirche im Mittelalterstil wußte Schinkel mit den eigenen Idealen in einem neuen Stil seiner »antikisierenden Gotik« zu vereinen. Die auf den ersten Blick neogotisch wirkende Architektur beinhaltet viele antikisierende Bauformen und Strukturen. Für die Außenarchitektur wählte Schinkel eine damals neuartige Materialästhetik, den sichtbaren Ziegel, während der Innenraum mit seiner Sandsteinimitation ein Werk des Pinsels ist. Auch das Gewölbe, das nur dem Kenner verrät, daß es sich hier um ein Kreuzgewölbe handelt, sieht mit seinem Ziegel imitierendem Anstrich, den aufgemalten Rippen und Lilienbändern wie ein sorgfältig aufgemauertes Sterngewölbe aus. Der fünfjochige Kirchenraum wirkt durch die nach innen gezogenen Strebepfeiler dreischiffig. Zwischen die Strebepfeiler setzte Schinkel spitzbogige Emporenarkaden aus Eiche, die den Raum einschließlich des Chorpolygons allseitig umfassen. Die Kirche wird seit 1987 als Museum genutzt. MAB

26–28. Berlin-Reinickendorf (Tegel), Karolinenstraße, Humboldtschlösschen, 1820–24

Das Schlösschen, seit 1766 im Besitz der Familie Humboldt, wurde in den Jahren 1820–24 von Schinkel umgebaut. Die Runderker der Eingangsseite stammen noch von dem Vorgängerbau. Schinkel fügte vier stark gegliederte Türme an, die über den obersten Fenstern acht Reliefs der Windgötter zeigen, von Rauch entworfen, aber doch eine Idee Schinkels. Die Vorderfront springt gegenüber den Türmen vor, die Gartenfront zurück, das Obergeschoß ist hier noch weiter zurückgenommen. Sowohl die Vorderfront als auch besonders die Gartenseite sind mit Fenstern reich gegliedert, letztere zeigt links und rechts vier Nischen mit Marmorkopien antiker Statuen, etwa der verwundeten Amazone. Die Figuren wurden 1836 aufgestellt. Die Dächer sind flach und mit Zinkplatten gedeckt. Im Erdgeschoß geht das Vestibül durch das ganze Haus, es sollte nach Schinkels Vorstellung auch als Gartensalon genutzt werden. Vor zwei dorischen Säulen steht ein antiker Pozzo, ein Brunnen, der an das Impluvium eines römischen Hauses erinnert und 1809 aus dem Kloster San Callisto in Rom erworben wurde. Das Haus beherbergt eine umfangreiche Antikensammlung, es

wird noch heute von den Nachfahren Humboldts bewohnt und hat im Kriege keinen Schaden genommen. HIB

29. Berlin-Reinickendorf (Tegel), Park des Humboldtschlösschens, Grabstätte, 1829

Am westlichen Ende der Wiesenfläche des Parks von Tegel liegt die Begräbnisstätte der Familie Humboldt und ihrer Nachfahren. Im Mittelpunkt einer halbkreisförmigen Exedra-Bank steht eine ionische Porphyrsäule mit einer Statue der Spes, der Hoffnung, von Thorvaldsen. Dies ist das Grabmal der Caroline von Humboldt, der Frau Wilhelm von Humboldts, die 1829 starb, das Grabmal selbst wurde von Schinkel entworfen. HIB

30. Berlin-Wedding, Pank-, Ecke Badstraße, Kirche St. Paul, 1832–34

Die Kirche gehört zu den vier Vorstadtkirchen in Berlin. Der Putzbau wird von weitständigen Pilastern mit korinthischen Kapitellen gegliedert. Im Gegensatz zu den beiden Vorstadtkirchen Nazarethkirche (Abb. 31, 32) und St. Johannis, die Formen der norditalienischen Romanik aufnehmen, orientieren sich die Kirchen St. Elisabeth und St. Paul an anti-ken Tempelformen. Die Apsis der Kirche St. Paul wurde 1885 angebaut, der Glockenturm 1889/90 angefügt, beide veränderten die ursprüngliche Konzeption. Die im Krieg zerstörte Kirche wurde 1957 wiederaufgebaut, wobei Hans Wolff-Grohmann das Innere völlig neu gestaltete. HIB

31, 32. Berlin-Wedding, Leopoldplatz, Nazarethkirche, 1832–34

Die Kirche gehört zu den vier Vorstadtkirchen in Berlin. Der unverputzte, ganz in Ziegeln ausgeführte Bau der Nazarethkirche zeigt unter einem flachen Giebel eine große Fensterrose und ein dreiteiliges Portal mit romanischen Bögen. Die Kirche besitzt, wie alle Vorstadtkirchen, keinen Turm. Die Südseite an der Schulstraße ist großzügig gegliedert mit kleinen Fenstern unten und großen oben über den ehemaligen Emporen. Diese Gliederung ist im Inneren der Kirche nicht mehr gegeben, weil 1906 eine Zwischendecke eingezogen wurde. Unten gibt es einen Kindergarten, oben werden die Gottesdienste abgehalten. Die flache Decke dieses oberen Raumes wurde Ende der siebziger Jahre gemäß den Schinkelschen Vorgaben restauriert und ausgemalt. HIB

33, 34. Berlin-Zehlendorf (Wannsee), Glienicke, Kleine Neugierde, 1825, und Große Neugierde, 1835

Schon 1796 hatte einer der vorgehenden Besitzer an der Stelle der heutigen Kleinen Neugierde ein Teehäuschen errichtet, von dem aus man den vorbeifließenden Verkehr zwischen Potsdam und Berlin besser als von den weiter hinten liegenden Gebäuden aus beobachten konnte. Schinkel baute ein Zimmer und eine sich zum Park öffnende Vorhalle mit ursprünglich dorischen Säulen, die 1847/48 durch eine florentinische Renaissance-Arkade ersetzt wurde. An den Wänden sind Spolien eingelassen. Die Ausmalung des Teezimmers existiert nicht mehr. Wenige Schritte westlich, in der Ecke des Parks nach Potsdam und zur Glienicker Brücke hin, liegt die Große Neugierde, ein von Säulen getragener Rundbau mit einem runden Aufsatz. Dieser Aufsatz ist eine Nachbildung des Lysikrates-Monuments in Athen, 334 v. Chr.

Schinkel baute die Große Neugierde 1835–37 nach Skizzen des Kronprinzen. Anlaß war die Einweihung der neuen Glienicker Brücke 1834 durch Alexandra, die Kaiserin von Russland, die Schwester Prinz Karls. Die Rotunde ist mit einem umlaufenden, vergoldeten Gitter geschmückt. 1907 wurde die Brücke erneuert, 1938 die Straße verbreitert, die Große Neugierde wurde deswegen erst gehoben, dann verschoben. HIB

35. Berlin-Zehlendorf (Wannsee), Glienicke, Schloß, 1825–28

Prinz Karl (1801–83), der drittälteste Sohn von Friedrich Wilhelm III. und Königin Luise, erwarb 1824 das Gut Klein Glienicke, das vorher schon durch viele Hände gegangen war, um dort einen Sommersitz südlicher Prägung zu errichten, womit Schinkel beauftragt wurde. Die Löwenfontäne, hart an der Straße, ist einem Vorbild an der Gartenfassade der Villa Medici in Rom nachempfunden, der Blick von hier zum Schloß ist heute leider fast zugewachsen. Das Schloß, bei dem Formen des Vorgängerbaus berücksichtigt werden mußten, ist ein schlichter klassizistischer Bau mit Putzquaderung und einem um Balkonbreite vorspringenden Mittelrisalit mit vier Pfeilern. Gegenüber diesem Gartenausgang befinden sich der Eingang und das Treppenhaus mit der wiederhergestellten linearen Bemalung und einem Geländer mit Messingstäben. Im ersten Stock liegt das sogenannte Weiße Zimmer oder auch Schinkelzimmer mit Gesims und Türrahmen aus weißem »stucco lustro« und einem geschwungenen Ecksofa. Runde Vertiefungen an den Wänden nehmen Büsten auf, im Bilde Prinzessin Marie von Preußen, die Gemahlin des Prinzen Karl. Der Hof wird auf der Nordostseite von einer Hecke und der Front des Kavalierhauses abgeriegelt, davor steht eine Kopie der Ildefonso-Gruppe, Sinnbild des Schlafes und des Todes. Zwischen den Fenstern sind zwei kolossale Marmormasken des römischen Theaters eingelassen. Dahinter erhebt sich ein Turm, den Schinkel 1832 anfügte und der 1865 um ein Geschoß erhöht wurde. Überall an den Wänden sind Spolien, Reste antiker Statuen und Kapitelle, eingelassen, die Prinz Karl sammelte. HIB

36, 37. Berlin-Zehlendorf (Wannsee), Glienicke, Kasino, 1824/25

Der wohlproportionierte Bau wurde 1824/25 von Schinkel als erstes der Glienicker Gebäude errichtet, es ist der Umbau eines alten Billardhäuschens. Die Putzgliederung betont die Horizontale, auf den Dachecken stehen große Schalen. Auffallendstes Element sind zwei Pergolen, die die Verbindung des Hauses zur Natur herstellen. An der Ostseite des Kasinos ist eine pompejanische Scheinarchitektur angebracht, vor der eine Exedrabank steht. Hier gab es früher ein pompejanisches Gärtchen. Im Inneren liegt, hinter einem Vorzimmer, der kleine Saal oder »Mittlere Salon« mit einer Feldereinteilung in Stuckmarmor und einem großen Metallüster. Der Raum wurde in den siebziger Jahren des 19. Jahrhunderts von Prinz Karl völlig umgestaltet. HIB

38. Berlin-Zehlendorf (Wannsee), Pfaueninsel, Schweizerhaus, 1829/30

Gleich links bergauf hinter der Anlegestelle liegt, unter Bäumen fast verborgen, das Schweizerhaus, das Schinkel 1829–30 als Gärtnerhaus baute. Es entsprach einer Mode der Zeit, der Sehnsucht nach dem Einfachen, Ländlichen. Das Schweizerhaus, geborgen im

Tal des Gebirges, wurde als ein Urtyp des Hauses oder Tempels empfunden, als Ur-Hütte. Die Putzritzung des Sockels täuscht eine Zyklopenmauer vor, Fenster- und Türrahmen und die Gesimse sind holzgeschnitzt und mit Rankenwerk und Palmetten bemalt. Die Eingangstreppe ist offen ins Haus gelegt, bündig mit der Hauswand stehen zwei Pfeiler, mit angedeuteten Kapitellen. Diese Eingangssituation, in all ihrer Bescheidenheit, erinnert an das Treppenhaus des Alten Museums (Abb. 12) als Verbindung von Innen und Außen. Die Dächer der Giebelwände kragen weit vor. HIB

39. Berlin-Zehlendorf (Wannsee), Pfaueninsel, Kavalierhaus, 1824–26

1823 wurde in der Brodbänkengasse in Danzig ein spätgotisches Patrizierhaus abgerissen, dessen Fassade der Kronprinz erwarb. Schinkel hatte die Aufgabe, diese Fassade einem in der Mitte der Insel gelegenen Wirtschaftsgebäude vorzublenden, einem 1804 von Friedrich Ludwig Carl Krüger erbauten Gutshaus. Dieses bestand aus einem Trakt zwischen zwei Türmen. Die Fassade wurde dem höheren, südlichen Turm vorgebaut, die Front des restlichen Gebäudes wurde im gotischen Stil umgestaltet und angepasst, so daß ein ebenso einheitliches wie eigentümliches Gebäude entstand. HIB

40. Potsdam, Pfingstberg, Pomona-Tempel, 1800 bis 1801

Der seit 1817 Pfingstberg genannte Hügel diente wie fast alle Anhöhen der Umgebung dem Obst- und Weinbau. Ein dort erwähnter »temple de Pomone« wurde 1800 durch einen Neubau ersetzt. Das im Mai 1801 fertiggestellte Bauwerk ist als frühester selbstständiger Bau Schinkels anzusehen. Seine Existenz schien durch Friedrich Wilhelms IV. Architekturphantasien auf dem Pfingstberg in Frage gestellt. Doch eine Reduzierung des Bauvorhabens und Lennés ausgeführter Gartenplan von 1862 sicherten ihm seine herausgehobene Stellung mit dem weiten Blick über Potsdam. In den letzten Jahrzehnten mutwillig zerstört, konnte der Bau nach 1990 aus den Resten zurückgewonnen werden. HSCH

41, 42. Potsdam, Alter Markt, Nikolaikirche, 1830–37

Ein Jahr nach dem Brand der Potsdamer Stadtkirche 1795 hatte Friedrich Gilly einen Neubau entworfen, der die Grundidee des Pantheons mit der Autonomie der Revolutionsarchitektur verband. Hinter der hohen Front mit vorgesetztem dorischen Portikus trat die flache Kuppel kaum in Erscheinung. Als Schinkel 1826–29 neu plante und sich mit dem Wunsch des Königs nach einer Zweiturm-Basilika auseinanderzusetzen hatte, bestärkte ihn der Kronprinz in der Kuppelgestalt. Schinkel übernahm in dem 1830 begonnenen Bau die großen Thermenfenster der Seitenfassaden und den Portikus, entschied sich jedoch für eine korinthische Ordnung. Er setzte die Zentralraumidee durch, veränderte aber Gillys arenenartiges Rund zum griechischen Kreuz. Obwohl die Pläne ausgearbeitet waren, konnten erst ab 1843 Persius und Stüler die Kuppel mit den aus statischen Gründen zugefügten vier Ecktürmen ausführen. Nach schweren Schäden am Ende des Zweiten Weltkriegs erhielt die Kirche 1953 bis 1960 eine neue Kuppel; der Außenbau mit dem Portikus wurde bis 1975 wiederhergestellt, das Innere bis 1981. HSCH

43–48. Potsdam, Sanssouci, Schloß Charlottenhof, 1826–29

1825 stand das kleine Bauerngut im Südwesten des Parkes Sanssouci zum Verkauf, das Johann Boumann d. Ä. erworben und ausgebaut hatte und das auch Johann Büring und Carl von Gontard eine Zeitlang besaßen. Peter Joseph Lenné erkannte die Gelegenheit, eine Ausdehnung des friderizianischen Gartens zu erreichen. Mit dem Erwerb des Anwesens durch die Krone legte er einen ersten Plan zur Neugestaltung vor, während Schinkel den Umbauauftrag für das Gutshaus erhielt. Der Kronprinz beteiligte sich als Bauherr mit über 100 Skizzen an der Planung. Er nannte Charlottenhof »mein Siam«, verstanden als Synonym für eine bessere Welt, und verfolgte damit die Absicht einer Selbstdarstellung seiner künftigen Herrschaftsform, die einen harmonischen Ausgleich aller Stände und Interessen anstrebte. Charlottenhof hat sich als einziges Werk Schinkels im Äußeren wie im Inneren vollständig erhalten, umgeben von der ebenso bewahrten und gepflegten Gartenlandschaft Lennés. Seit der Gründung der Schlösserverwaltung im Jahr 1927 ist es als Museum öffentlich zugänglich. HSCH

49–53. Potsdam, Sanssouci, Römische Bäder, 1829–39

Ab 1829 entstand im Anschluß an das Schloß Charlottenhof ein Etablissement für den Hofgärtner. Als bewußter Gegensatz trat neben die feste Orthogonale des Schloßbezirks die freie Entfaltung einer »mannigfaltigen Gruppe architektonischer Gegenstände« mit der Gärtnerwohnung im »Stil italienischer Landgebäude« als Mittelpunkt. Um den Turm dieser »Villa«, der ein Wasserreservoir und ein Badekabinett aufnahm, reihen sich ein Stallgebäude mit darüberliegender Wohnung des Gehilfen, eine Arkadenhalle, deren Dach der weiten Aussicht über die Gartengrenzen hinweg dient, ein tempelförmiger Teepavillon für den Kronprinzen und die alles vereinende Große Laube. Die Brunnennische hinter der Arkadenhalle wandelte sich in einem zweiten Schritt zu einem antiken Vestibül mit nachfolgendem Impluvium, dem in drei Konchen endenden Apodyterium und einem Caldarium mit vertieftem Badebecken unter einem Oberlicht. Allein auf diesen letzten Teil der Anlage, eine spielerische Adaption der durch aktuelle Grabungen in Pompeji vermittelten Kenntnisse römischen Hausbaus, geht die heutige, die gesamte Anlage umfassende Bezeichnung »Römische Bäder« zurück. HSCH

S. 16

C. Brand, Karl Friedrich Schinkel, 1832.

Katalog Ludwig Persius
Alle Texte von Hillert Ibbeken

1, 2. Berlin-Zehlendorf, Park Glienicke, Jägertor, 1842/43
Das Tor liegt am nördlichsten Punkt der Glienicker Parkanlage nur wenige hundert Meter westlich des Gasthauses Moorlake und gegenüber der Heilandskirche von Sacrow (Abb. 34, 35). Die Flanken bilden zwei rechtwinklig zueinander geführte und leicht abknickende Mauern mit je zwei Pfeilern mit Dreipässen und Fialen, die Mauern sind zinnenbewehrt. Das westliche Mauerende umhüllt einen großen Findling. Die beiden Mauern berühren sich jedoch nicht, sondern geben in der Mitte dem eigentlichen Torbau Raum. Seine Ecken werden von vier schlanken, oktogonalen Säulen gefasst, die hohe Zinnenkronen tragen. Das Mauerwerk ist ziegelsichtig. Durch das Tor gelangt man zu dem 1828 von Schinkel im Stil der englischen Gotik erbauten Jägerhof. Persius zitiert dessen Motiv mit einem flach gespannten Tudorbogen über der Durchfahrt, sie trägt ein Kreuzrippengewölbe. Über der linken, östlichen Nebenpforte ist ein Renaissance-Wappen eingemauert, das Prinz Carl vermutlich erst später erwarb. Unter dem Zinnenkranz verläuft ein Fries aus Formsteinen, die Außenseite des Tores schmücken zwei Adlerwappen.

3. Berlin-Zehlendorf, Park Glienicke, Maschinen- und Gärtnerhaus, 1838
Das Maschinen- und Gärtnerhaus liegt, den zum Wasser hin abfallenden Hang überspannend, ein wenig nördlich des Schlosses Glienicke an der Havel. Das Gebäude ist der erste selbständig von Persius errichtete Bau für den Prinzen Carl. Er verbindet die technischen Anforderungen eines Pumpenhauses und Wasserreservoirs ideal mit denen der Garten- und Parkästhetik. Rein technisch wäre es günstiger gewesen, den Turm mit dem Reservoir oben auf dem Hang anzulegen, weil damit ein höherer Wasserdruck möglich gewesen wäre, ein so dominantes Gebäude hätte die Harmonie des Parkes und seiner Gebäude jedoch empfindlich gestört. So steht der fünfgeschossige, tief gegründete Turm unten am Hangfuß, daran links angeschlossen liegt, halb verborgen, das eigentliche Dampfmaschinen-Häuschen , das bis 1952 eine 18 PS starke Pumpe der Firma Egells barg. Den Turm gliedern ein Balkon, eine Reihe von Schlitzfenstern, eine dreifache Arkade im Belvedere-Geschoß und eine abschließende Arkadenreihe vor dem Impluviumdach. Zwischen diesem und dem Belvedere befand sich der mit Kupferblech ausgeschlagene Wasserspeicher, der von oben mit Regenwasser und von unten mit dem heraufgepumpten Wasser gefüllt wurde. Der 25 m hohe Turm, ein statisches Meisterwerk, wird im Inneren von vier Pfeilern durchzogen, Schornstein und alle Rohre sind nach innen verlegt. Auf der Hochfläche liegt das Gärtnerhaus, ein Umbau eines kleinen Vorgängerbaus. Es handelt sich um einen schlichten Quader mit fein profilierten Fensterfaschen, der die Reihe von Schlitzfenstern des Turmes wieder aufnimmt. Eine zweigeteilte Pergola führt zu dem Gebäude, zweigeteilt, weil der eigentliche Pergola-Gang nicht bis zum Eingang durchgezogen ist, sondern dort in eine quadratische Eingangspergola mit Pfeilern und zwei Säulen mündet. Dadurch entsteht eine reiche Gliederung. Wesentliches architektonisches Element des Ensembles ist der hohe Bogen, der auf der Mitte des Hanges den Turm unten mit dem Gärtnerhaus oben verbindet. Persius greift hier ein von Schinkel häufig gebrauchtes Motiv der Verbindung von Turm und Gebäude auf, so etwa bei dessen Kirchen in Müncheberg, Petzow oder Krummöls (Schlesien). Abgesehen von dem ästhetischen Reiz einer solchen Konstruktion, ergibt sich oft die Notwendigkeit, bei schlechtem Baugrund die höhere Setzung eines schweren Turmes mit kleiner Grundfläche gegenüber dem restlichen Gebäude abzufangen.

4. Berlin-Zehlendorf, Schloß Glienicke, Wirtschaftshof, 1845
Der Wirtschaftshof liegt praktisch unmittelbar an der Straße Potsdam–Berlin, von Berlin kommend ganz kurz vor der Einfahrt zum Schloß. Auffallendstes Element der Gebäudegruppe ist der durch einen hohen Bogen getrennte Kuh- und Pferdestall mit einem Turm. Das Motiv des Bogens als Verbindung zweier Gebäudeteile wurde von Persius öfter angewandt, so bei dem nahegelegenen Maschinen- und Gärtnerhaus oder der Meierei im Park Sanssouci. Auch Schinkel verwendete es oft. Der ursprünglich gedrungene Turm wurde von Petzholtz 1872 aufgestockt; ob der Ochsenkopf mit Baldachin noch von Persius entworfen wurde, ist nicht bekannt. Die Gebäudegruppe wurde erst nach dem Tode von Persius ausgeführt. Unmittelbar an der Straße liegt ein kleines, ehemals als Konditorei errichtetes Gebäude. Das zweigeschossige Haus mit einer kleinen Eingangspergola ist glatt verputzt. Drei doppelte Rundbogenfenster auf der langen Seite, zwei auf der schmalen gliedern das obere Stockwerk; die Kämpfer verbindet ein fein profiliertes Gesims. Das Rundbogenmotiv wird von dem überdachten Schornstein übernommen.

5. Berlin-Zehlendorf, Schloß Glienicke, Südostflügel, 1844
Betritt man das Schloßgelände von der Straße Berlin–Potsdam kommend, trifft man zuerst auf die Südostecke des Schlosses. Dieser Gebäudeteil wurde im Sommer 1844 von Persius aufgestockt, als die prinzliche Familie auf einer längeren Italienreise weilte. Im selben Flügel lagen auch die Zimmer der Hofdamen und der drei Kinder des Prinzenpaars. Die Attika über einem schmalen Gesims trägt die gleiche Putzquaderung wie das untere Stockwerk. Die Löwengestalten aus Zinkguß an den Mittelpfeilern der Fenster werden auch auf Persius zurückgeführt.

6. Berlin-Zehlendorf, Schloß Glienicke, Portikus, 1840
Persius schmückte den neuen Zugang zum Schloß am Ostflügel mit einem Portikus aus dorischen Säulen und Pfeilern auf attischen Basen. Das Dach ziert, von oben nach unten gesehen, ein Palmettenkranz auf der Traufe, darunter ein Eierstab und dann ein reich bewegter Figurenfries mit hingelagerten Frauengestalten, einem auf einem Delphin reitenden Putto und einer über eine Art Seekuh hingestreckten Frau. Dieser Figurenfries soll auf Schinkel zurückgehen. Darunter folgt ein blattartiger Fries und zuunterst ein Astragal, eine Perlenschnur mit dazwischengeschalteten Plättchen. Das Ganze besteht aus Zinkguß der Firma Geiß und wurde 1840 geliefert.

7, 8. Berlin-Zehlendorf, Schloß Glienicke, Stibadium, 1840
Das Stibadium liegt an der Südseite des Schlosses Glienicke und grenzt den Garten nach Osten zum Zufahrtsweg hin ab. Die Exedra, die sich nach Westen hin, mit Blick auf Potsdam, öffnet, wird von einem Velum, einem nach Art eines Segels gerafften Holzdach überdacht, die Felder der Decke sind mit Arabesken und Götterdarstellungen bemalt. Das Dach ruht im Halbkreis auf acht kleinen dorischen Säulen auf der hinteren Mauer; im Mittelpunkt des radialstrahligen Daches stand ursprünglich eine Karyatide von Kiß aus Zinkguß, die später durch diese Figur aus Marmor ersetzt wurde. Möglicherweise handelt es sich bei diesem Stibadium auch um ein römisches Zitat, weil Plinius d. Ä. berichtet, bei seinem Landsitz gäbe es ein Stibadium, unter dem Wasser aus Röhren flösse, und gegenüber läge ein Springbrunnen, eine Situation, die auch auf Glienicke zutrifft, wo ein mit einem Löwenkopf gefasster Quell unter dem Stibadium fließt. Wichtig ist die Sichtachse aus dem Stibadium nach Westen, nach Potsdam, die durch die heutige Vegetation beeinträchtigt ist.

9. Bornim, Max-Eyth-Allee, Amtsturm, 1844/45
Der Amtsturm liegt etwa 1,5 km nördlich der Ortschaft Bornim bei Potsdam, auf einem flachen Hügel ein wenig oberhalb des nördlich gelegenen Sacrow-Paretzer-Kanals und des Fahrlander Sees. Der Turm und das anschließende Mäuerchen sind das einzige Überbleibsel, der klägliche Rest eines stattlichen und komplexen Oekonomie-Gehöfts, das in den Jahren 1844/45, also ganz kurz vor seinem Tode, von Persius entworfen und errichtet wurde. Das Gehöft ging nach dem Einmarsch der Roten Armee 1945 in Flammen auf, die Reste wurden 1956 bis 1961 beseitigt, nur der Turm und das Mäuerchen blieben erhalten. Der Turm diente seinerzeit auch zur Kontrolle der Bediensteten auf den Feldern des Betriebs, heute trägt er eine Mobilfunkantenne. Er ist in gelbem Backstein ausgeführt, auf jede vierte Lage folgt ein Durchschuß von grünlichem Backstein. Einziger Schmuck neben drei schmalen Fensterschlitzen auf jeder Seite ist eine Loggia mit vier Öffnungen und Rundbögen und einem schmalen, um den Turm herumgeführten Kämpferband. In den Brüstungsmauern der Loggia kehrt das Motiv der Aussparungen des Mäuerchens wieder. Der Turm war ursprünglich durch einen Gang mit drei Arkaden mit dem Amtshaus verbunden, im Turmsockel ist die vierte, jetzt zugemauerte Arkade erhalten.

10. Bornstedt, Eichenallee / Amundsenstraße, Bornstedter Durchstich, 1843/44
Der Bornstedter Durchstich, ein Wassergraben, liegt westlich von Bornstedt nahe dem Wegeschnittpunkt Eichenallee/Amundsenstraße. Friedrich Wilhelm IV. beauftragte Persius mit dem Entwurf einer Brücke in Form eines römische Viadukts. Vier hohe Pfeiler tragen die Rundbögen, die Brücke ist aus Rüdersdorfer Kalkstein gemauert. Die ursprüngliche gemauerte Brüstung war verfallen und wurde deshalb bei der Instandsetzung 1997 bis 1999 durch ein hölzernes Geländer ersetzt.

11, 12. Potsdam, Park Babelsberg, Maschinenhaus, 1843/44
Das Maschinenhaus liegt unterhalb des Schlosses Babelsberg unmittelbar am Wasser, an der Glienicker

Lake, genau in der Sichtachse von der Pergola des Schlosses zum Schäferberg, wo damals an der Stelle des heutigen Postturms ein Semaphor stand. Das Maschinenhaus ist ein Blickfang für alle, die vom Haupteingang des Parkes kommen. Auftraggeber war Prinz Wilhelm, der auch für die Babelsberger Anlagen Fontänen wünschte. Bauleiter war M. Gottgetreu, auf den auch spätere Umbauten zurückgehen. Persius lehnte sich stilistisch an den von Schinkel vorgegebenen »normannischen« Stil des Schlosses Babelsberg an, er verwendete keine Rundbogenfenster und bewehrte den ganzen Bau mit Zinnen. Ein Turm mit quadratischem Umriß korrespondiert diagonal gegenüber an der anderen Gebäudeecke mit dem sehr dominanten, runden Schornstein, auf dem ein schlanker, achteckiger Abschlußturm steht. Den Schornstein schmückt ein Spiralband aus grün glasierten Ziegeln. Mehrere kubische Baukörper sind asymmetrisch aneinandergefügt und mit kleinen Erkertürmchen verziert. Alle Dächer sind Impluviumdächer. Die Maschinenhalle wurde von einem Oberlicht erhellt. Überraschenderweise war die Wohnung des Maschinenmeisters mit der Halle vereint, auch befanden sich im Obergeschoß Gästezimmer. Die 40 PS starke Dampfmaschine, die die vor dem Seeufer angebrachte Fontäne auf fast 41 m Höhe trieb, war so leise, daß sie die unterschiedliche Nutzung des Hauses erlaubte.Um die Unregelmäßigkeiten der handgestrichenen Ziegel im Mauerwerk auszugleichen, wurde der Mörtel der Fugen mit einer halbrund ausgekehlten Fugenkelle glattgezogen, so daß ein ebenmäßiges Mauerbild entstand.

13–16. Potsdam, Park Babelsberg, Schloß, 1844–49

Das Schloß liegt in beherrschender Lage auf dem Babelsberg über der Glienicker Lake. In einer ersten Bauphase baute Schinkel 1835–37 den östlichen Teil der Baugruppe für den Prinzen Wilhelm unter der Bauleitung von Persius. Die zweite Bauphase, 1844–49, in der der westliche Komplex entstand, beruht weitgehend auf Entwürfen von Persius. Beherrschendes Element sind das hohe Oktogon des Tanzsaals im Osten und die Fahnenturmgruppe im Westen. Dazwischen liegen unregelmäßige, vor- und rückspringende Glieder mit Balkonen und Erkern, reich gegliedert durch Gesimse, Fenster im Tudorstil, Friese und Strebepfeiler. Der Bau ist überwiegend ziegelsichtig ausgeführt. Der Tanzsaal im großen Oktogon (Abb. 15, 16) erstreckt sich über die beiden unteren Geschosse, darüber liegen Dienerzimmer, auch mit Blick in den südlichen Park. Das Oktogon, zinnenbewehrt wie alle Teile des Schlosses, ist hochdifferenziert gestaltet, mit verschiedenen Friesen, Fensterformen und Fenstereinfassungen.

17, 18. Potsdam, Am Grünen Gitter 3, Friedenskirche, 1844–48

Die Friedenskirche liegt, zusammen mit dem Marlygarten und dem von Lenné angelegten Teich am äußersten Ostrand des Parkes von Sanssouci. Friedrich Wilhelm IV. bestimmte die Basilika von San Clemente in Rom als Vorbild, auch sollte die Kirche ein mittelalterliches Mosaik von San Cipriano auf Murano aufnehmen, das er 1835 erworben hatte. Der Sockel besteht aus Rüdersdorfer Kalkstein und einer Ziegelschicht, der eigentliche Baukörper hat Putzquaderung, wobei unterschiedliche Farbtöne unterschiedliche Sandsteinquader

vortäuschen. Das flach geneigte Zinkdach ist mit Akroteren geschmückt. Die dreischiffige Kirche besitzt eine Haupt- und zwei Nebenapsiden, die sich im Wasser spiegeln. Die Traufe der Hauptapsis ist über einem Konsolband mit Palmetten geschmückt. Der hohe Turm mit sechs offenen Geschossen und gekuppelten Drillingsarkaden zitiert den Turm von Santa Maria in Cosmedin in Rom. Der Kirche vorgelagert zum Marlygarten hin liegt ein Atrium, eine offene Halle mit dorischen Säulen und attischen Basen, an der Kirchenseite mit ionischen Kapitellen, wie sie auch im Inneren zu finden sind. Das Atrium öffnet sich mit einer doppelten Arkadenreihe sehr malerisch zum Marlygarten. Das Innere, durch Obergadenfenster gut beleuchtet, zeigt die offene Holzkonstruktion der Decke; die Säulen mit ionischen Kapitellen aus Zinkguß bestehen aus dunklem Marmor aus dem Harz. Nach dem Tod von Persius wurde der Kirchenbau von L. F. Hesse und F. von Arnim unter der Bauleitung von A. Stüler zu Ende geführt.

19. Potsdam, Am Neuen Garten 10, Meierei, 1843/44

Die Meierei liegt am äußersten nördlichen Ende des Neuen Gartens unmittelbar am Jungfernsee. Der Kern des Hauses war 1790–92 als Ökonomiegebäude in neogotischem Stil errichtet worden, von C. G. Langhans entworfen, ausgeführt von A. L. Krüger. Persius erhöhte den Bau um ein Geschoß und fügte in der südwestlichen Ecke einen Turm auf quadratischem Grundriß an. Die südöstliche Gebäudeecke wird durch drei spitzbogige Fenster gegliedert. Die Zinnen sind mit Terrakotta-Steinen geschmückt, darunter liegt ein Konsolfries. 1862 wurde der Meiereibetrieb eingestellt und ein Maschinenhaus gebaut, weshalb auch der Schornstein errichtet werden mußte. Das Gebäude wird seit 2003 von einer Brauerei-Gaststätte bewirtschaftet.

20. Potsdam, Breite Straße 28, »Moschee«, Dampfmaschinenhaus für Park Sanssouci, 1841 bis 1843

Das Dampfmaschinenhaus von Sanssouci, die sogenannte »Moschee«, liegt unmittelbar an der Neustädter Havelbucht. Es ist dies zweifellos das eigenwilligste Gebäude von Persius. Die Stilvorgabe »nach Art der türkischen Moschee« stammt von Friedrich Wilhelm IV., und der Maschinenbauer Borsig sorgte für die technische Ausrüstung, assistiert von A. Brix als Mechaniker und M. Gottgetreu als Bauleiter. Ziel des Bauvorhabens war, für die Wasserkünste von Sanssouci eine leistungsfähige Pumpmaschine in einem malerischen Maschinenhaus zu schaffen, weil man zu Recht befürchtete, ein reiner Zweckbau würde die Gegend verschandeln. Stilvorgabe waren schließlich keine türkischen, sondern Kairoer Architekturen, der Innenraum ist der Moschee von Cordoba und der Alhambra nachempfunden. Der Außenbau besticht durch die klaren geometrischen Formen aneinandergerückter Kuben, gekrönt von einer steilen Kuppel über einem oktogonalen Unterbau und einem Tambour mit Rundbogenfenstern. Unmittelbar daneben steht, als Minarett ausgeführt, der Schornstein. Vielfarbig glasierte Ziegelreihen betonen die Horizontale des Gebäudes. Über der Brüstung des unteren Abschnitts des Minaretts erhebt sich ein oktogonaler mittlerer Teil mit großer Zickzack-Bänderung. Die Spitze des Minaretts bilden gußeiserne, wie ziseliert wirkende Arkaden und ein Halbmond. Im Inneren stehen die 80 PS starke Dampfmaschine und das Pumpenwerk, eine

verwirrend vielfältige Anlage von Stangen, Hebeln und Rädern, eingefügt in die Pfeilerstrukturen mit Kleeblattbögen und reichen Kapitellen, alles aus Gußeisen und bunt bemalt, beleuchtet durch die fensterreiche Kuppel. Von hier wird noch heute, allerdings mit unauffälligen, modernen Elektropumpen, das Wasser auf den Ruinenberg nördlich des Schlosses Sanssouci gepumpt, um von dort die Fontänen des Parkes zu speisen. Ein Schauspiel, das zu betrachten Friedrich dem Großen versagt war, weil es die damalige Technik noch nicht erlaubte.

21. Potsdam, Park Sanssouci, Kastellanshaus, 1840/41

Das Kastellanshaus schließt die Schloßanlage von Sanssouci nach Osten ab. Das untere Geschoß, an den Hang gelehnt, wurde nach Art einer Felsgrotte 1788 errichtet. Friedrich Wilhelm IV. wünschte eine Aufstockung, um Wohnraum für die Hofbediensteten zu schaffen. Persius behielt die axiale Gliederung des Sockels bei und fügte nördlich und südlich zwei Kopfbauten an, wenig vorspringende Risalite mit drei gekuppelten Bogenfenstern. Die Mittelachse des Baues betont eine Ädikula von F. von Arnim, die erst 1847 angefügt wurde. Unter dem wenig vorspringenden, relativ flachen Dach liegt ein Konsolfries. Der südliche Kopfbau diente als Billardzimmer – mit Blick auf die Kuppel der Gemäldegalerie.

22. Potsdam, Leipziger Straße 7/8, Proviantamt mit Körnermagazin, 1844/45

Das Proviantamt mit dem Körnermagazin liegt an der Leipziger Straße zwischen dem Brauhausberg und der Havel. Der große barocke Vorgängerbau besaß ein Walmdach; er wurde, von der Wasserseite und dem Lustgarten aus gesehen, als landschaftsprägender Blickfang den Wünschen von Friedrich Wilhelm IV. nicht gerecht. Er beauftragte Persius mit der Verschönerung der Fassade. Bei dem viergeschossigen Bau wechseln Rundbogen- und Rechteckfenster ab; das Attikageschoß der gesamten Anlage ist mit Zinnen bekrönt. Den Bau überragt ein hoher Turm im »normannischen« Stil mit vier Erkern an den Ecken. Das Gebäude steht heute leer und verfällt.

23–25. Potsdam, Park Sanssouci, Fasanerie, 1842–44

Die Fasanerie liegt am Südrand des Parkes Sanssouci zwischen dem Bahnhof Wildpark und dem Schloß Charlottenhof. Da die Hofjagdgebiete in den Wildpark verlegt worden waren, wünschte Friedrich Wilhelm IV. dort die Anlage von Förstereien, den sogenannten Etablissements, und einer Fasanerie, die die Verbindung zum Park Sanssouci und dem Schloß Charlottenhof bilden sollte. Die dazugehörenden Gartenanlagen wurden von Lenné entworfen. Persius konnte bei der Fasanerie den Stil der italienischen Villa mit Turm und kunstvoll arrangierten Kuben voll entfalten, ohne Elemente von Vorgängerbauten übernehmen zu müssen. Die perfekte horizontale und vertikale Gliederung der Gebäudegruppe erzielt ihre Wirkung nach allen Seiten. Der Bau war sowohl als Funktionsbau für die Fasanenhaltung als auch als Wohnung für zwei Angestellte und ihre Familien gedacht. Die südliche Loggia mit zwei Faunen am Gitter war als Teeplatz für den König eingerichtet. Die Fasanerie dient heute als Wohnhaus.

26, 27. Potsdam, Park Sanssouci, Hofgärtnerhaus, 1829–32

Das Hofgärtnerhaus gehört zur Baugruppe der Römischen Bäder, es liegt zwischen Charlottenhof und der Handtmannschen Meierei im Südosten des Parkes Sanssouci. Bei diesem von Schinkel entworfenen und ausgeführten Gebäude war Persius als Baukondukteur eng eingebunden. Es ist dies sozusagen die Urzelle der italienischen Villa in der Potsdamer Architekturlandschaft: ein aufgelockerter Gebäudekomplex mit vielfältigen, angeschobenen Kuben, relativ flachen, weit vorkragenden Dächern, Fenstern im Rundbogenstil und einem Turm. Persius übernahm diesen von Schinkel geprägten Bautypus und gestaltete ihn in den zahlreichen Varianten seiner Potsdamer Villen. Das Haus wird heute als Wohnhaus und für Ausstellungen genutzt.

28. Potsdam, Park Sanssouci, Ruinenberg, Normannischer Turm, 1845/46

Der Normannische Turm steht auf dem Ruinenberg in der nördlichen Sichtachse des Schlosses von Sanssouci. Hier stand bereits eine Ruinenstaffage aus dem Wandfragment eines römischen Zirkus, einem dorischen Rundtempel und drei ionischen Säulen, die sich in einem großen Wasserbecken spiegeln, dem Reservoir für die Wasserspiele des Parkes. Der König wünschte hier einen Aussichtsturm, um den von Lenné gestalteten Landschaftspark überblicken zu können, auch ein Teezimmer sollte eingerichtet werden. Der von Persius vorgelegte Entwurf fand die Billigung des Königs, der Turm wurde nach Persius' Tod von F. von Arnim in Kalkbruchstein aus Rüdersdorf ausgeführt. Der Turm lehnt sich unmittelbar an die Zirkuswand und ist mit einer Zinnenkrone geschmückt.

29. Potsdam, Park Sanssouci, Ruinenberg, Exedra, 1843/44

Die Exedra liegt an der westlichen Flanke des Ruinenbergs gegenüber dem Krongut Bornstedt. Die halbrunde Bank mit Greifenfüßen als Armlehnen ist von der Bank vor dem Grab der Priesterin Mamia an der Gräberstraße in Pompeji abgeleitet, auf der Goethe 1787 bei seinem Besuch in der Campagna saß. Friedrich Wilhelm IV. ließ an vielen landschaftlich markanten Stellen derartige Bänke aufstellen. Die Photographie versucht, ein Aquarell von Carl Graeb nachzustellen.

30, 31. Potsdam, Park Sanssouci, Schloß Sanssouci, Erweiterungsbauten, 1840–42

Die Erweiterungsbauten schließen sich westlich und östlich unmittelbar an das Schloß Sanssouci an. Ihre Anlage war notwendig geworden, weil die Vorgängerbauten für die erweiterte Hofhaltung von Friedrich Wilhelm IV. nicht genügend Raum boten. Die langgestreckten, um mehrere Achsen erweiterten Gebäude sind der Nordfassade des Schlosses mit seinen korinthischen Pilastern so geschickt angepaßt, daß sie kaum als Neubauten wirken. Die Stirnseiten schmücken Vorhallen mit drei Bögen. Im östlichen Anbau sind die Küche, die Backstube und der Weinkeller untergebracht, die oberen Räume dienen dem Küchenpersonal. Die Küche mit dem original erhaltenen Herd sowie den gußeisernen Säulen und Deckenträgern geht auf Entwürfe von Persius zurück; ausgeführt wurden sie von F. v. Arnim. Im westlichen Erweiterungsbau, dem Damenflügel, wohnten die Hofdamen und Kavaliere. Die Räume sind durch Treppenhäuser an den Enden des Baues erschlossen, Korridore gibt es nicht, sondern eine Enfilade in beiden Geschossen. Die Gestaltung der Traumzimmer geht, wie der Name verrät, auf einen Traum von Friedrich Wilhelm IV. zurück, das Tapetenzimmer im Obergeschoß besitzt ein Oberlicht. Der Damenflügel wurde erstmals mit Wassertoiletten ausgestattet.

32. Potsdam, Maulbeerallee, Stibadium im Paradiesgärtlein, 1841–48

Das Stibadium liegt wenig westlich unterhalb des Orangerieschlosses an der Maulbeerallee im botanischen Garten. Das Stibadium oder Atrium, ein Ort der Kontemplation, ist ein quadratischer, oben offener Bau mit einem Impluviumdach, ganz wie bei den Römischen Bädern von Schinkel. Ein westlicher Anbau endet in einer halbrunden Apsis, im Norden und Süden finden sich Portale und an der Ostseite eine Ädikula. Das den Bau nach oben abschließende Gebälk, ein Triglyphen-Metopenfries, trägt kein Dach, sondern setzt im Gegenteil auf dem schmalen inneren Dachkranz auf. Das Geviert des zentralen Bassins umgibt eine Reihung von Terrakottasäulen mit korinthischen Kapitellen. Im Bassin steht eine Plastik von F. L. Bürde (1846) mit einem großen Adler, der ein Reh schlägt. Der westliche Nebenraum besitzt eine schwere Kassettendecke, die Apsis schmücken pompejanische Motive mit Hermen, Vögeln und Girlanden. Das Stibadium entstand in enger Zusammenarbeit mit dem König.

33. Potsdam, Am Grünen Gitter 5/6, Villa Illaire, 1843–46

Die Villa Illaire liegt am am östlichen Ende des Parkes Sanssouci. Der eingeschossige Vorgängerbau aus dem 18. Jahrhundert wurde vom Hofgärtner Sello, danach vom Hofgärtner Voß bewohnt. Persius entwarf auf Wunsch des Königs einen Umbau für den Kabinettsrat Illaire. Es entstand eine reich gegliederte Baugruppe mit unterschiedlich hohen, flachen Impluviumdächern. Nur das Sockelgeschoß trägt eine Putzquaderung, das Obergeschoss, glatt verputzt, gliedern scharf eingeschnittene Rechteckfenster mit Zinkgußfiguren an den Oberfenstern. Nur an der Straßenfront findet sich ein großes Rundbogenfenster über dem Balkon, ein Thermenfenster, mit stämmigen Putti als Karyatiden. Eine Pergola schafft die Verbindung zu dem westlich vorgelagerten Gehilfenhaus. Die relativ strenge Nordseite zum Schloß hin schmückt ein auf ausdrücklichen Wunsch von Friedrich Wilhelm IV. angebrachtes Ädikulafenster. Die einzelnen Körper des zentralen Baues verbindet ein markanter Konsolfries direkt unter der Traufe. Im östlich angrenzenden Marlygarten wurde ein Teich angelegt.

34, 35. Sacrow, Krampitzer Straße, Heilandskirche, 1843/44

Die Sacrower Kirche, noch zu Potsdam gehörend, liegt unmittelbar am Ufer der Havel, die sich hier, von der Pfaueninsel kommend, zum Jungfernsee erweitert. Diese Kirche ist vielleicht das berühmteste Gebäude von Persius. Sie geht auf eine Ideenskizze von Friedrich Wilhelm IV. zurück, der auch den Bauplatz bestimmte. Der König besuchte den Bau oft und ordnete viele Einzelheiten an. Von außen, besonders vom gegenüberliegenden Ufer aus, wirkt der Bau wie eine dreischiffige Basilika. Dieser Eindruck entsteht durch die die Kirche vollständig umgebende Arkadenhalle mit Rundbögen. Die Säulen sind aus Sandstein, die Kapitelle aus Zinkguß. Über den Arkaden liegt ein mächtiger Konsolfries mit Palmetten. Der ganze Bau ist mit Backstein verblendet und von Lagen blau glasierter Ziegel mit Rosetten durchschossen, die die Horizontale der Kirche betonen. Fünf scheinbare Obergadenfenster mit Rundbögen geben der Kirche Licht, die westliche Giebelseite besitzt neben dem Eingang nur eine Fensterrose. Ein großer, rechteckiger Vorplatz wird im Norden durch den frei stehenden Campanile begrenzt, im Süden durch eine Rundbank mit einem Hochkreuz. Das schlichte Innere der Kirche wird von dem offenen Dachstuhl mit Holzgebälk und den sehr hoch liegenden Fenstern bestimmt, zwischen denen holzgeschnitzte Apostelfiguren von J. Alberty stehen. Die Ausmalung der Apsis stammt von C. Begas. Die die Fensterrose umgebende Orgel der Eingangsseite ist eine Attrappe. Die Kirche, unmittelbar im Grenzgebiet der ehemaligen DDR gelegen, war zeitweise sehr gefährdet, konnte aber vollständig wiederhergerichtet werde.

S. 62
F. Jentzen, Ludwig Persius, um 1843.

Katalog Friedrich August Stüler

Die Katalogtexte sind gekürzte Fassungen von Texten aus: Eva Börsch-Supan und Dietrich Müller-Stüler *Friedrich August Stüler, 1800–1865*, Deutscher Kunstverlag, München und Berlin 1997, ergänzt durch eigene Bemerkungen von Hillert Ibbeken.

1, 2. Berlin-Charlottenburg, Spandauer Damm / Ecke Schloßstraße, ehemalige Garde-du-Corps-Kasernen, 1851–59

Der König wünschte 1844 den Bau zweier Kasernen gegenüber dem Charlottenburger Schloß. Komplikationen beim Grundstückskauf ließen den Bau erst 1851 beginnen, 1859 wurde er abgeschlossen. Der klar gegliederte Kubus liefert von allen Seiten den gleichen Anblick. Der Bau ist siebenachsig, die mittleren drei Achsen springen als Risalit geringfügig vor und werden von Giebeln abgeschlossen, die die umlaufende Balustrade unterbrechen. Der Sockel des dreigeschossigen Baues ist gequadert, die beiden oberen Stockwerke sind glatt verputzt und mit Pilastern gegliedert, die in korinthischen Kapitellen mit Adlern und ausgebreiteten Flügeln enden. Ein Konsolgesims und ein Band mit kreisförmigen Fenstern schließt den Bau nach oben ab. Beherrschendes Element ist eine zentrale Kuppel auf dem Dach, die den Bezug zum Schloß herstellen soll und vermutlich nicht auf Stüler zurückgeht. Sechzehn Säulen mit korinthischen Kapitellen aus Terrakotta der Firma March tragen einen Fries mit Blattwerk und Helmen, darüber spannt sich die gerippte Halbkugel der Kuppel. Das im Krieg beschädigte Gebäude wurde in den 1950er Jahren wiederhergestellt, es beherbergt heute das Museum Berggruen. Die Abbildungen zeigen das westliche der beiden ganz gleichartigen Gebäude.

3–5. Berlin-Marzahn, Alt Marzahn, ev. Dorfkirche, 1870/71

Die Kirche wurde schon 1857 entworfen, sie ersetzt die abgerissene Feldsteinkirche aus dem 13. Jahrhundert, eine von über fünfzig alten Berliner Dorfkirchen. Der gut erhaltene und gepflegte gelbe Backsteinbau ist sehr klein, mit fünf Achsen; markante Strebepfeiler bestimmen das Äußere. An der Chorseite erhebt sich ein hoher Staffelgiebel, auch die Turmgiebel über einer einfachen Doppelarkade sind gestaffelt. Unter dem Traufgesims liegt ein einfaches, gekreuztes Schmuckband aus Formziegeln. Der kleine, angeschobene Chor ist rechteckig. Im Innern überraschen ein weitgespanntes Kreuzrippengewölbe sowie eine sorgfältig restaurierte Hufeisenempore auf schmalen Ständern, die sechs Arkaden bilden. Die Kirche ist in vorzüglichem Zustand, jedoch wurde bei der Restaurierung 1962 und 1982/83 die ursprüngliche Ausstattung zerstört.

6, 7. Berlin-Mitte, Bodestr. 3, Alte Nationalgalerie, 1867–76

Der Bau wurde 1867–76 von Johann Heinrich Strack ausgeführt, also nach dem Tode von Stüler, der das Gebäude 1862–65 entworfen und dabei Skizzen von Friedrich Wilhelm IV. berücksichtigt hatte. Dem Baugedanken liegt der Entwurf Friedrich Gillys für ein Denkmal Friedrichs des Großen zugrunde, für den sich 1797 der damals sechzehnjährige Schinkel so sehr begeistert hatte. Der tempelartige Oberbau auf 12 m hohem Sockel in Gestalt eines römischen Pseudoperipteros hat eine gewollte und gelungene städtebauliche Fernsicht. Die Stirnseite ist von frei stehenden korinthischen

Säulen geprägt, an den übrigen Fronten sind es korinthische Halbsäulen, zwischen denen die Namen deutscher Künstler eingemeißelt sind. Die Fenster sind nur wenig betont. Dies ist nach dem Brandenburger Tor der erste Werksteinbau in Berlin. Das Relief des Frontgiebels zeigt Germania als Beschützerin der Künste, darüber die Gruppe der drei bildenden Künste von Rudolf Schweinitz auf dem Giebel. Dem Gebäude vorgeschaltet ist eine große, doppelläufige Freitreppe, zwischen deren Wangen im Erdgeschoß der rundbogige Eingang liegt. Darüber erhebt sich das Reiterstandbild von Friedrich Wilhelm IV., eine Bronzearbeit von Alexander Calandrelli, 1882. Die Rückseite zeigt eine Exedra über die ganze Höhe der Nationalgalerie. Den oberen Abschluß bilden ein reich bewegter, wellenartiger Bildfries und ein Konsolsims unter einem Palmettenfries. Das Gebäude wurde im Krieg schwer beschädigt und schon in den 1950er Jahren wiederhergerichtet, eine weitere Restaurierung reichte bis 2001. Von der Stülerschen Innenarchitektur hat sich nichts erhalten. Das Gebäude ist in sehr gutem Zustand.

8, 9. Berlin-Mitte, Bodestr. 4, Neues Museum, 1843 bis 1846, 1855, 1865

Die Abbildungen aus dem Neuen Museum geben den ruinösen Zustand im Mai 2003 wieder, sie lassen die alte Pracht nur erahnen. Das klassizistische Gebäude in Schinkelscher Tradition ist das wichtigste Bauwerk von Friedrich Wilhelm IV. und, neben dem Nationalmuseum in Stockholm und der Akademie in Budapest, das Hauptwerk von Stüler. 1841 entworfen, wurde es 1843 bis 1846 gebaut und wegen der Revolution von 1848 erst 1855 vollendet, die Ausmalung des Treppenhauses erst 1865. Die Museumsinsel, in ihrem Nordteil überwiegend Hafengelände, wurde mit diesem Bau zu einer großartigen Museumslandschaft erweitert. Dies verlangten die gewachsenen Sammlungen und ein gesteigertes Interesse für weitere Kunstgebiete. Wie das Alte Museum gruppiert sich auch das Neue Museum um zwei Innenhöfe. Der Mittelteil ist von Giebeln mit reichen figürlichen Darstellungen gekrönt, die Seitenrisalite tragen Kuppeln mit innen zweigeschossigen Rotunden. Der schlechte Baugrund verlangte ein leichtes Gebäude mit andererseits großer Tragkraft für schwere Exponate. Stüler löste dieses Problem höchst professionell und elegant mit weitgespannten Eisenkonstruktionen, den ersten ihrer Art in einem Großbau in Berlin, sowie mit Gewölben, die aus hohlen Töpfen gemauert wurden. Die Ruine, ein trauriger Vorteil, läßt diese Bauelemente deutlich erkennen. Alle Räume waren in ihrer Architektur und Ausmalung auf die jeweiligen Exponate abgestellt.

10, 11. Berlin-Pankow, Breite Straße, ev. Dorfkirche, 1857–59

Bei dieser Kirche handelt es sich um einen Erweiterungsbau, der an eine mittelalterliche Kirche angeschlossen ist. Die alte Kirche wird als Chor benutzt, die neue ist dreischiffig mit höherem und breiterem Mittelschiff. Dieses Dreiermotiv wird in dem Durchbruch zum Chor wieder aufgenommen, wo zwei niedrigere und schmalere neben dem höheren zentralen Bogen stehen. Ein an der Ostwand des Chores abgesetzter breiter Bogen erweckt innen den Eindruck einer Apsis, die es jedoch nicht gibt. Taufstein und Kanzel sind erhalten, letztere zeigt die Kirchenlehrer, darunter Luther, Zinzendorf und Calvin. Zwei hohe, achteckige Chorflankentürme betonen die Grenze zwischen alter und neuer Kirche.

1908 wurde eine große Vorhalle mit zwei Nebengebäuden vor die Westseite gesetzt, die den Bau harmonisch abschließt. Die Kirche ist innen und außen in vorzüglichem Zustand.

12, 13. Berlin-Tiergarten, Alt-Moabit 25, ev. Kirche St. Johannis, 1851–57

Die Johanniskirche ist eine der von Schinkel gebauten Vorstadtkirchen, 1833–35. Die Gemeinde wünschte schon früh ein Pfarrhaus. Nach einigen Entwurfsänderungen baute Stüler 1851–53 das Pfarr- und Schulhaus, 1856 die Arkadenhalle und 1856/57 den Turm, der zur Zeit der photographischen Aufnahme für eine Renovierung eingerüstet war. Die elfachsige Arkadenhalle zeigt in der Mitte vor dem Haupteingang der Kirche eine große Vorhalle mit einem Christuskopf und zwei schwebenden Engeln im Giebel, getragen von zwei korinthischen Säulen vor ebensolchen Pilastern. An den Seiten vier Nischen mit Figuren der Evangelisten. Die Arkadenhalle ist gut erhalten.

14, 15. Berlin-Tiergarten, Matthäikirchplatz, ev. Kirche St. Matthäus, 1844–46

Der 1843 gegründete Kirchenbauverein beauftragte Stüler mit einem Entwurf, der König übernahm das Patronat. Die Kirche ist eine dreischiffige Halle, die Seitenschiffe werden von kleineren Apsiden abgeschlossen, das Mittelschiff von einer höheren und größeren Apsis. An den Seiten des sechsachsigen Baues finden sich im Erdgeschoß jeweils kleine rundbogige Fensterpaare, im oberen Geschoß sowie an den Giebelseiten sind es Dreierfenster, deren mittleres etwas erhöht ist. Der eingestellte Turm an der Nordseite ist etwas schmaler als das Mittelschiff. Unter seiner achteckigen Spitze liegt ein Arkadenumgang, den vier Ecktürmchen begleiten, die aus den Lisenen hervorgehen. Durch schmale Nischen, die die Regenrohre aufnehmen, sind die Giebelfronten klar voneinander getrennt. Der ziegelsichtige Bau mit gelben Blendziegeln ist mit horizontalen roten Streifen und einem Sims unter den oberen Fenstern klar gegliedert, die zentrale Apsis und die Giebel zieren Rundfenster. Die Kirche wurde kurz vor Kriegsende stark zerstört und 1956–60 im äußeren Bild wiederhergestellt, sie ist vorzüglich erhalten. Das zerstörte Innere wurde vollständig verändert, es hat allerdings eine hervorragende Akustik und wird gerne zu Konzerten benutzt. Eine fast identische, aber etwas kleinere Stülerkirche steht in Peitz nördlich von Cottbus. Die Matthäuskirche ist in sehr gutem Zustand.

16, 17. Berlin-Zehlendorf, ev. Kirche St. Peter und Paul auf Nikolskoe, 1834–37

Der erste Anstoß zum Bau dieser Kirche war der romantische Wunsch der Zarin, auf der Pfaueninsel Kirchenglocken läuten zu hören. Der König entschied sich für einen Entwurf Stülers, auch Vorschläge des Kronprinzen wurden aufgenommen. Die Kirche liegt auf dem relativ steilen Hang des Havelufers gegenüber dem südwestlichen Ende der Pfaueninsel, was eine hohe Aufsockelung auf der Nordostseite erforderlich machte, auf die auch der hohe Querriegel verweist. Er trägt einen zentralen, erst vier-, dann achteckigen Turm mit reich verzierter Kuppel. Der Turm wird von zwei seitlichen, dreifachen Arkadenhallen flankiert, die das berühmte Geläut der Kirche bergen. Eine große, zentrale Fensterrose enthält auch eine Uhr. Die Lisenen an den Ecken des Querriegels sind ein wenig über das Dach hinausgezogen, ganz wie bei der Kirche von Christdorf, die der Nikolskoer Kirche sehr ähnelt . Der hohe Saalbau hat vier Rundbogenfenster und eine Apsis mit fünf Rundfenstern. Der rückwärtige Giebel ist mit dunkelroten Ziegelquadraten geschmückt, ein umlaufender Sims umgibt fast die gesamte Kirche. Unter dem hölzernen Vorbau im russischen Stil liegt das große Portal, dessen Archivolte mit Terrakotta-Steinen mit pflanzlichen Motiven ausgelegt ist. Das gesamte ziegelsichtige Mauerwerk der Kirche ist äußerst akkurat ausgeführt. Ebenso gut ist das Innere der Kirche in der originalen Ausstattung erhalten. Die tief gegliederte Kassettendecke korrespondiert mit den Brüstungen der Emporen, die das gesamte Schiff umziehen. Der große Triumphbogen vor der Apsis findet seinen Widerpart in dem ebenso großen Bogen der Orgelnische. In den Zwickeln der Bögen sind vier Tondi mit den Evangelisten gemalt. Die Kapitelle der achteckigen, schlanken Emporenpfeiler sind wie Bildstöcke gehalten, mit Engelsbildern und Akanthusblättern. Eine Besonderheit ist die hohe Kanzel auf vier Pfeilern mit korinthischen Kapitellen und geflügelten Engelsköpfen. Am Korb finden sich ovale Mosaiken mit Petrus und Paulus. Gegenüber der Kanzel auf gleicher Höhe befand sich die Hofloge. Die Kirche ist ganz vorzüglich erhalten.

18, 19. Berlin-Zehlendorf, Wilhelmplatz, ev. Dorfkirche am Stölpchensee, 1858/59

Auf einem Hügel über dem Stölpchensee, in beherrschender Lage, steht die kreuzförmige Kirche im Rundbogenstil, ein Auftrag an Stüler durch den König. Der mächtige Turm über der Vierung trägt, wie alle anderen Bauteile, Lisenen an den Ecken, die hier in Fialen übergehen. Chor und Querschiff sind als fünfteilige Konchen angelagert, das einschiffige Langhaus besitzt drei Achsen, auch seine Wände sind durch Lisenen gegliedert. Das gelbe, ziegelsichtige Mauerwerk mit roten, horizontalen Streifen ist vorzüglich erhalten. Die Westfassade zeigt eine große Fensterrose nach romanischem, italienischem Vorbild. Im Innern entwickeln sich die Bögen der Vierung ohne Kämpfer aus den Pfeilern. Bei der Restaurierung Anfang der 1990er Jahre wurde statt einer leichten, sandsteinfarbenen Quaderbemalung der Raum komplett geweißt und damit ein ungünstiger Kontrast zu den zu dunkel gestrichenen Decken erzeugt. Die Balkendecke des Langhauses ist flach, die der Vierung und der Konchen relativ steil. Die achteckige Kanzel auf schlanken Säulen zeigt stehende Apostelfiguren. Die Kirche besitzt ein prächtiges Grabmal der Hofgärtnerfamilie Heydert von 1777. Sie ist sehr gut erhalten.

20, 21. Caputh, Straße der Einheit, ev. Kirche, 1850 bis 1852

Caputh liegt etwas südlich von Potsdam am Templiner und Schwielow-See. Die Kirche steht ganz in der Nähe des kurfürstlichen, frühbarocken Schlosses. Ein Umbauentwurf der Regierung Potsdam war vom König abgelehnt worden, der Stüler mit einem neuen Entwurf beauftragte und auf Details, so die Gestaltung des Turmes, Einfluß nahm. Die Kirche ist eine dreischiffige, fünfjochige Emporenbasilika im Stil der italienischen Romanik, etwa San Zeno in Verona. Auf Wunsch des Königs wurden Teile der Mauern des Vorgängerbaus beibehalten. Die reich gegliederte südwestliche Fassade zeigt Putzquaderwerk mit gelbem Ziegelwerk an den Lisenen und Gebäudeecken. Im Hauptgiebel liegt eine große

Fensterrose, der kleine Giebel der Vorhalle hat fünffache Rundbogenfenster, zur Mitte hin ansteigend. An der Nordwestseite, zur Straße hin, erhebt sich der hohe, frei stehende Campanile, mit dem Schiff durch eine kleine Zwischenhalle mit einer Sakristei verbunden. Der Turm, im Sockel viereckig, geht in einen achteckigen Teil über, dessen Ecklisenen den Bau deutlich gliedern. Darüber ein flacher Helm mit Kreuz. Im Innern werden die Arkaden von Pfeilern mit schlanken Ecksäulen, bekrönt von Würfelkapitellchen, getragen, die kassettierte Decke ist flach. Der Orgelprospekt ist original erhalten, vor der Apsis wölbt sich ein großer Triumphbogen mit einem Spruchband. Die beiden großen Kronleuchter sind über sinnreiche Seilzüge und Rollen miteinander verbunden. Die Kirche wurde nach der Wende vorzüglich renoviert und ist sehr gut erhalten.

22. Caputh, Marienquelle, 1855

Der Entwurf der Quellfassung geht auf eine Anregung des Königs zurück, der das Grab der Maria im Kidrontal bei Jerusalem als Vorlage wünschte. Die Marienquelle liegt etwa 400 m nördlich vom Ortsende seitlich der Uferstraße, recht einsam im dichten Wald, davor der Quelltümpel, der keine Fassungen mehr erkennen läßt. Der Bau besteht aus einer schlichten, gelben Ziegelmauer mit seitlichen, niedrigeren Fortsätzen und drei übereinandergestaffelten, weiten Spitzbögen aus roten Ziegeln, die an sarazenische Formen erinnern. Die beiden äußeren Bögen werden von vier Säulen getragen, hinter dem inneren Bogen mit dem eigentlichen Quelldurchlaß liegt ein ausgeputztes Quadrat, in dessen Zwickeln zwei Tondi mit zerstörten Reliefs angebracht sind. Die Marienquelle wurde vor einigen Jahren renoviert, auch eine spätere, arge Verunzierung durch Graffitti wurde entfernt.

23, 24. Potsdam, Park Sanssouci, Orangerieschloß 1850–60

Friedrich Wilhelm IV. plante schon als Kronprinz, begeistert von den Villen in der Umgebung Roms, den Hügel nordwestlich von Sanssouci mit einer Anlage aus Orangeriehallen und Schloß beziehungsweise Villa zu krönen. Unter den wechselnden römischen Vorbildern war auch Raffaels unvollendete Villa Madama. Ab 1840 schuf Persius Entwürfe mit einem Mittelbau, der ein Theater enthielt, seit 1847 erscheint in den Skizzen des Königs als grundlegendes Gestaltungselement das »Palladiomotiv« (Mittelbogen, seitlich gerades Gebälk). Im April 1850, nachdem der Pfingstbergentwurf vollendet war, schuf Stüler in drei Entwürfen, die der König jeweils veränderte, die gültige Baugestalt: Mittelbau mit Vorhof, Zweiturmriegel zwischen Kolonnaden (mit weitem Blick über Sanssouci), Orangenhallen durch breite Pfeiler rhythmisiert, schmale, aber tiefe Seitengebäude. Diese öffnen mit Palladio-Bogen die 300 m lange Terrasse und den Blick von der Heilig-Geist-Kirche bis zum Belvedere – die »Direktionslinie« der geplanten Höhenstraße, deren glanzvoller Abschluß die Orangerie sein sollte, in der Mittelarkade das Standbild Friedrich Wilhelms IV. von Gustav Bläser, 1873.

25–27. Potsdam, Ribbeckstraße, ev. Kirche, 1855/ 1856

Für die Kirche gab es einen Vorentwurf von Ludwig Persius sowie mehrere Entwürfe von Stüler. Als besonders problematisch erwies sich ihre Ausrichtung auf den Friedhof, da möglichst wenige Gräber zerstört werden

sollten. Die Kirche im Rundbogenstil ist ein vierachsiger Saalbau mit gelben Verblendziegeln aus Joachimsthal. Die Ecken tragen Baldachine mit Apostelfiguren aus Terrakotta. Die Westseite mit dem Eingang als Giebelportal ist mit einer großen Fensterrose und einem kleinen Glockenstuhl auf dem Giebel geschmückt. Die Seiten des Langhauses haben je drei gekuppelte Rundbogenfenster zwischen den Lisenen. Im Osten wurde 1881–83 ein Chor durch Reinhold Persius, den Sohn von Ludwig Persius, angebaut. Die Balkendecke im Innern ist flach und sehr dunkel, das gilt auch für die Emporen, die auf quer gestellten hölzernen Arkaden ruhen. Da sich unter den Emporen keine Fenster befinden, ist die Kirche relativ dunkel. Zur Straße hin ist die Kirche durch einen neunfachen Arkadengang mit Rundbögen und Giebeldach abgeschlossen. Er wird im Süden von einem einachsigen kleinen Kopfbau, im Norden durch den großen Campanile abgeschlossen. Der Arkadengang hat zur Straße hin eine Brüstung aus engständigen Doppelsäulchen mit Kapitellchen und Rundbögen. Der Turm ist mit wenig vortretenden Ecklisenen und einer Mittellisene gegliedert und zeigt jeweils zwei Rundbogenfenster in jedem der fünf Geschosse. Sein Dach ist ein flaches Pyramidendach über einem Rundbogengesims. Die Kirche wurde 1977–81 restauriert und ist sehr gut erhalten, wegen des nahen Kronguts Bornstedt wird sie viel besucht.

28. Potsdam, Schopenhauerstraße, Weinbergstor, 1850/51

Stüler machte zwei Entwürfe und verarbeitete mehrere Skizzen des Königs, der hier, am geplanten Abzweig der Höhenstraße von der damaligen Bornstedter Allee, einen Triumphbogen wie den der Geldwechsler in Rom wünschte. Auf der Rückseite des Architravs wird des niedergeschlagenen Aufruhrs in der Rhein-Pfalz und in Baden gedacht, auf der Vorderseite unverfänglich nur das Baudatum 1851 genannt. Die Terrakotta-Platten wurden von March und Feilner hergestellt, sie zeigen an der Vorderseite die vier Kardinaltugenden: links Stärke und Gerechtigkeit, rechts Mäßigkeit und Klugheit, darunter als Liegefiguren Symbole der Telegraphie und der Eisenbahn, auf der Rückseite entsprechend die Künste. An den inneren Laibungen finden sich der Auszug und die Wiederkehr der Truppen. Das Bauwerk ist in gutem Zustand.

S. 98

A. Menzel, Friedrich August Stüler, 1861/62.

Catalogue Karl Friedrich Schinkel

MAB   Martina Abri
HIB   Hillert Ibbeken
HSCH Heinz Schönemann

1. Berlin Charlottenburg, Gierkeplatz, Luisenkirche, 1823–26

The church was renovated by Schinkel in 1823–26. He redesigned the interior and added a tower. The church was burnt out in 1943, and Schinkel's work in the interior was not restored in the 1950–56 renovation, and so only the present tower is by Schinkel. It has three storeys, and the windows and decorative bands are the same in all three. The name Luisenkirche refers to Queen Luise, who was unusually popular with the people. HIB

2. Berlin-Charlottenburg, Schloss Charlottenburg, bedroom of Queen Luise, 1810

Queen Luise came back to Berlin with the king from exile in Memel in December 1809, but then died in July 1810. It was in this short period that Schinkel designed what is possibly his most famous piece of furniture, the queen's ship bed, the »lit bateau«, one of his first creations for the royal family. The narrow sides end in the volutes of Ionic capitals, and are exactly the same, so that the head and the foot cannot be identified as such, and each carries a bolster. The long side of the light birchwood bed is framed by a flowing garland ending in fluttering bands. Previously the two small flower tables probably carried glass or silver washing vessels. The walls are structured by falling, gathered folds of white muslin, an almost transparent cotton fabric through which the pink of the wallpaper shimmers as a symbol of the dawn. HIB

3, 4. Berlin-Charlottenburg, park of Schloss Charlottenburg, Mausoleum, 1810–12

Immediately after the death of Queen Luise in July 1810 the king made a sketch of the mausoleum in which he wanted to bury his consort. Schinkel realized this design and built a portico with four columns in sandstone, which was replaced by red granite, the rock »of the fatherland« in 1828. The sandstone portico was re-erected on the Pfaueninsel. Heinrich Gentz designed the interior of the mausoleum. It contained, alone at first, the queen's marble sarcophagus, created by Christian Daniel Rauch in 1811–14. The queen is portrayed sleeping, in a garment with many pleats. The base with coat-of-arms and eagle goes back to Schinkel's work, and so do the two large candelabra. One was executed by Friedrich Tieck, the other is also by Rauch. In 1840, on the death of Friedrich Wilhelm III, the mausoleum was enlarged, and the king's marble sarcophagus was erected in 1846. HIB

5, 6. Berlin-Charlottenburg, park of Schloss Charlottenburg, Neuer Pavillon, 1824/25

This building, also called the Schinkelpavillon, was commissioned by Friedrich Wilhelm III in 1824/25 so that he could live in it with his second consort, whom he married morganatically. It stands in the south-eastern corner of the park, at the top of the path that leads behind the Schloss. The building is modelled on the royal Casina del Chiatomone near Naples, which no longer exists; the king had stayed there in 1822. The building is almost cubic, and completely surrounded by a delicate balcony on the first floor. Each of the four sides is re-

lieved by large loggias creating a clear connection between inside and outside, as in the Altes Museum, for example (ill. 13), the Schweizerhaus on the Pfaueninsel (ill. 38) or the Gesellschaftshaus in Magdeburg. Coming from the park, the view is flanked by two granite columns with bronze Victories by Christian Daniel Rauch, set up in 1840. The southern look is reinforced by palms in tubs. The most important room in the interior is the garden room. This has a large, semicircular wall niche, which Schinkel modelled on the round bench of the Priestess Mammia in the Street of Tombs in Pompeii. A generously draped wall hanging spans the semicircle, in blue fabric with gold edging and stars. In the middle is a raised marble figure carrying a bowl. The Neuer Pavillon was burnt out in 1943, and was completely restored in 1957–70. HIB

7, 8. Berlin-Kreuzberg, Viktoriapark, Kreuzbergdenkmal, 1818–21

As with the Friedrichswerdersche Kirche and the Neue Wache, there were many preliminary designs that differed from the final form taken by the Kreuzbergdenkmal. The version that was finally accepted was an obelisk-like tower reminiscent of polygonal Gothic spires, with numerous pinnacles and an iron cross on the top. The Kreuzbergdenkmal is a national memorial to the victories in the Wars of Liberation. The monument is just under 20 metres high, painted dark green, and rises on a cruciform ground plan. Around it are 12 niches, dedicated to 12 battles. The niches contain 12 genii, modelled by Christian Daniel Rauch, Friedrich Tieck and Ludwig Wichmann. Their heads are portraits of members of the royal household and army commanders, including Tsar Alexander I of Russia. The monument was raised by 8 metres in 1878, and placed on a plinth by Johann Heinrich Strack, so that it remained visible from a distance. Restoration in 1980–83 was not as successful as hoped, so that further and more thorough work was needed in 1996. This included the plinth, and was completed in September 2000, devouring 7 million marks. The original monument, the work of the Berlin Royal Iron Foundry, whose casting quality is praised by modern specialists, cost 78,365 thalers at the time it was made. HIB

9–11. Berlin-Mitte, Gendarmenmarkt, Schauspielhaus, 1818–21

The theatre built by the elder Langhans caught fire during a rehearsal for Schiller's Die Räuber on 29 July 1817 and burned down. Friedrich Wilhelm III commissioned a new building from Schinkel on 30 April 1818, which was to use the old foundations to as large an extent as possible. Schinkel built a tripartite complex in 1818–21, containing a theatre, a concert hall and storage and rehearsal space. The axis of the central section is set at right angles to the axis of the Gendarmenmarkt, while the two side sections are set on that axis. The building is almost fully fenestrated, with no round arches. The two upper storeys are articulated with pilasters, the lower storey for the storerooms and the heating plant forms a high plinth, spanned by a steep flight of outdoor steps in front of the central section. Above the steps is a portico with an Ionic columns and a lavishly decorated pediment. This tells the story of the Niobides as the symbol of tragedy. The pediment is repeated on the façade of the higher building housing the stage, and here the naked, winged Eros stands before a throne. This gable

is crowned by Apollo on a gryphon-drawn carriage. The nine Muses stand on the corners of the roof. The Schauspielhaus was burnt out completely at the end of the war, and next to nothing of the elaborate interior survived. Rebuilding finished in 1984, and the building is now used only as a concert hall. HIB

12–16. Berlin-Mitte, Lustgarten, Altes Museum, 1823–29

After the victories over Napoleon the stolen art treasures came back to Berlin, but there were no suitable exhibition galleries, and the expanding royal collections also faced this problem. Schinkel produced a plan for a new museum by the Lustgarten in 1822, opposite the royal Schloss, and this was accepted by Friedrich Wilhelm III on condition that the costs did not exceed 700,000 thalers. Building started in 1823 and went on until 1829, the opening was in 1830. The impressive architecture with a broad Ionic colonnade opening on to the Lustgarten and the Schloss, now demolished, is in keeping with the impressive site in the city centre. The four-winged complex is grouped around a central section that is higher than the rest of the building and contains a domed hall rising through both storeys: the rotunda, based on the Pantheon in Rome. The building is reached by a wide flight of steps in front of it, leading to an open stairwell that links the inside and outside of the museum together in a most felicitous manner. Unfortunately this effect is currently somewhat impaired by a glass screen hung between the inner columns, though this is to be removed. The museum was burnt out in the war and the exterior was restored by 1966. It presently houses an antiquities collection on the ground floor and exhibition galleries on the upper floor. HIB

17. Berlin-Mitte, Altes Museum, granite shell in the Lustgarten, 1827–34

The bowl is just under 7 metres in diameter and weighs about 1600 hundredweight. It is made of granite, the »rock of the Fatherland«, as it was called at the time, working on the erroneous assumption that there were outcrops of granite in Brandenburg as well. Ice-age origins as glacial deposits from Scandinavia were not accepted at the time. The gigantic block that the bowl was carved from was found by the Berlin building inspector Cantian. It was one of the so-called Markgrafensteine in the Rauen Hills near Fürstenwalde, where its remains can still be admired today. The bowl was roughly carved out on the spot and shipped to Berlin along the Spree, in a specially constructed barge. Schinkel wanted to place it in the rotunda of the Altes Museum there, but distanced himself from this idea when the bowl turned out to be even larger than originally planned. So it was placed in front of the outside steps to the museum, still a technological wonder, and by far the largest of its kind. HIB

18, 19. Berlin-Mitte, Oberwallstaße, details of the former Bauakademie, 1832–36

The Bauakademie, Schinkel's modern functional building, was burnt out in 1945, and the ruins were removed in 1962 to make room for the GDR Foreign Ministry. But many of the decorative elements of the building have survived, including parts of the main portals, which were placed adjacent to each other, the left-hand one leading into the General Building School and the right-hand one into the Trade School. The jambs of the left-hand entrance were set up together with the right-hand portal in the Schinkelklause behind the Kronprinzenpalais. With one exception the terra-cotta slabs modelled by August Kiss from drawings by Schinkel were placed correctly. The slabs provide a symbolic narrative of the development of architecture. The third image from the bottom on the right shows a kneeling girl with a foliage basket of ears of corn: the Corinthian mode; its counterpart on the right-hand side symbolizes the Ionic mode. Top left is Orpheus with his lyre, top right Amphion, who built the fortress of seven-gated Thebes with the sound of his lyre, an allusion to the combined efforts of architecture and music. The seven slabs in the lintel in between show genii towering up out of acanthus. The door-leaves carry portrait heads of master builders and sculptors, including Brunelleschi, who built the dome of Florence cathedral. The left-hand portal was shown at an exhibition in the Technische Universität Berlin, also with the heads of famous masters, including Raphael, named as R. Urbino. No decision has yet been taken about whether to rebuild the Bauakademie. At the time of writing the Bildungsverein Bautechnik is erecting one corner of the building as a sample façade, intended for completion in spring 2001. HIB

20. Berlin-Mitte, Unter den Linden, Neue Wache, 1817/18

The Neue Wache was Schinkel's first state commission after the Napoleonic Wars. After various preliminary designs, the king decided on the design that was »approximately based on a Roman castrum«. The Neue Wache is a cube on a square ground plan and is placed in a little chestnut grove between the Humboldt University and the Zeughaus, the current Deutsches Historisches Museum. The street façade of the rendered brick building forms a deeply staggered Doric columned portico in Saxon sandstone, whose pediment was created from 1842–46 by August Kiss to designs by Schinkel. The Neue Wache stood empty after the November Revolution of 1918 until Heinrich Tessenow transformed it into a memorial for the dead of the First World War in 1931. The open courtyard was roofed at this stage. The Neue Wache has been Germany's central memorial site since 1993. HIB

21–23. Berlin-Mitte, Unter den Linden, Schloßbrücke, 1821–24

Schinkel wrote: »The former Hundebrücke by the Zeughaus was a conventional wooden pile bridge that looked most inappropriate in the company of such imposing buildings as the Zeughaus and the royal Schloss, cramping and disfiguring this incomparably beautiful street in the most unseemly manner…« The king ordered the construction of a wide and handsome bridge that was not to disrupt the traffic in the street or on the river. Schinkel designed and built a bridge with three arches crossing the river diagonally, with four pedestals on each side. The marble figures are »completely idealized« representations of heroes and victory goddesses: »A young hero led into battle by a goddess of victory, a hero crowned by her, a hero in battle supported by her, a dying hero in her arms and the like.« This makes the bridge into another monument to the Wars of Liberation. The cast-iron railing with heavy parapet slabs, made by the Royal Iron Foundry, show alternate tritons and sea-horses, arranged alternately. HIB

24, 25. Berlin-Mitte, Werderstraße, Friedrichswerdersche Kirche, 1824–30

As the first prestigious brick building the Friedrichswerdersche Kirche is particularly important today, as it is Schinkel's only public building in Berlin that has survived intact both inside and out. Schinkel was able to combine the king's desire for a church in the medieval style with his own ideals in a new version of his »Gothic modelled on the ancients« The architecture looks neo-Gothic at first glance, but contains many building forms and structures copied from antiquity. Schinkel chose a material aesthetic that was new at the time for the exterior, unrendered brick, while the interior is imitation sandstone created by a paintbrush. The vaults would only reveal to a connoisseur's eye that they are cross vaults, as their paint imitating brickwork, their painted ribs and bands of lilies look like carefully built stellar vaulting. The interior with its five bays gives the impression of a nave and two aisles because of the drawn-in buttresses. Schinkel placed pointed gallery arches in oak between the buttresses, running round the space, including the choir polygon, on all sides. The church has been used as a museum since 1987. MAB

26–28. Berlin-Reinickendorf (Tegel), Karolinenstraße, Humboldtschlösschen, 1820–24

This Schlösschen, or little palace, had been in the Humboldt family since 1766, and was rebuilt by Schinkel in 1820–24. The round bay windows on the entrance side are from the earlier building. Schinkel added four strongly articulated towers showing eight reliefs of the wind gods above the topmost windows, designed by Rauch, but at Schinkel's suggestion. The front façade projects beyond the towers, while the garden façade is set back from them, and here the upper storey is taken even further back. Both the front façade and the garden side in particular are lavishly articulated with windows, and the latter has four niches on the right and left with marble copies of ancient statues, of the wounded Amazon, for example. The figures were put in place in 1836. The roofs are flat, and covered with zinc sheets. The vestibule runs through the whole building on the ground floor; Schinkel's idea was that it should also be used as a garden room. An ancient pozzo, a well reminiscent of the impluvium in a Roman house, stands in front of two Doric columns; it was acquired from the monastery of San Callisto in Rome in 1809. The building contains a large collection of antiquities and Humboldt's descendants still live in it. It was not damaged in the war. HIB

29. Berlin-Reinickendorf (Tegel), park of the Humboldtschlösschen, burial place, 1829

The burial palace of the Humboldt family and their descendants is at the western end of the grassy area in Tegel park. An Ionic porphyry column with a statue of Spes, Hope, by Thorvaldsen, stands at the centre of a semicircular exedra bench. This is the tomb of Caroline von Humboldt, the wife of Wilhelm von Humboldt, who died in 1829. The tomb was designed by Schinkel. HIB

30. Berlin-Wedding, junction of Pankstraße and Badstraße, church of St. Paul, 1832–34

This is one of the four suburban or Vorstadt churches in Berlin. The rendered building is articulated with widely-spaced pilasters with Corinthian capitals. Unlike the Nazarethkirche (ill. 31, 32) and St. Johannis, which adopt northern Italian Romanesque forms, the churches

of St. Elisabeth and St. Paul follow the form of ancient temples. The apse of the church of St. Paul was added in 1885, the bell-tower in 1889/90, and both change the original conception. The church was destroyed in the war and rebuilt in 1957, when the interior was completely redesigned by Hans Wolff-Grohmann. HIB

31, 32. Berlin-Wedding, Leopoldplatz, Nazarethkirche, 1832–34

This is one of the four suburban or Vorstadt churches in Berlin. The unrendered, completely brick structure of the Nazarethkirche has a rose window under a shallow pediment and a tripartite portal with Romanesque arches. Like all the Vorstadt churches it has no tower. The south side in Schulstraße is lavishly articulated with small windows below and large ones above the former galleries. This articulation no longer affects the interior of the church, as an intermediate ceiling was inserted in 1906. The downstairs rooms are used by a kindergarten, and services are held upstairs. The flat ceiling of the upper room was restored and painted in accordance with Schinkel's requirements in the late seventies. HIB

33, 34. Berlin-Zehlendorf (Wannsee), Glienicke, Kleine Neugierde, 1825, and Große Neugierde, 1835

One of the previous owners had built a little tea-house on the site of the present Kleine Neugierde as early as 1796. They had a better view from here of the traffic on the Berlin–Potsdam road – the name means »Little Curiosity« – than they did from the main buildings, which were set further back. Schinkel built one room and a portico opening on to the park. This originally had Doric columns, which were replaced by a Florentine Renaissance arcade in 1847/48. Spoils are set into the walls. The tea-room paintwork has not survived. A few steps to the west, in the corner of the park nearest to Potsdam and the Glienicke Bridge, is the Grosse Neugierde, a circular structure supported on columns with a round top section. This top was copied from the Lysicrates monument in Athens, 334 BC. Schinkel built the Grosse Neugierde in 1835–37 using sketches by the crown prince. The occasion was the opening of the Glienicke Bridge by Alexandra, the Tsarina of Russia and sister to Prince Karl. The rotunda is decorated with a continuous gilded grille. The bridge was rebuilt in 1907, and the road widened in 1938, so the Grosse Neugierde was first raised, then moved. HIB

35. Berlin-Zehlendorf (Wannsee), Glienicke, Schloss, 1825–28

The Klein Glienicke estate had passed through a large number of hands before Prince Karl (1801–1883), the third-eldest son of Friedrich Wilhelm III and Queen Luise, acquired it in 1824 to build a summer residence in the southern style, which was commissioned from Schinkel. The Lion Fountain, close by the road, is based on an original in the garden façade of the Villa Medici in Rome; the view from here to the Schloss is unfortunately almost completely overgrown now. The Schloss, for which some features had to be taken over from the earlier building, is a plain neoclassical building with rendered ashlar patterning and a central section with four piers projecting by the width of the balcony. Opposite this garden exit are the entrance and the staircase with the restored linear paintwork and a banister with brass bars. The White Room, also known as the Schinkel Room, is on the first floor. It has a cornice and door frame in white »stucco lustro« and a curved corner sofa. Round niches in the walls accommodate busts; our picture shows Princess Marie of Prussia, Prince Karl's wife. The courtyard is bordered on the north side by a hedge and the façade of the Kavalierhaus, and in front of this is a copy of the Ildefonso group, symbolizing sleep and death. Two colossal marble masks from the Roman theatre are set in between the windows. Behind is a tower that Schinkel added in 1832, raised by one storey in 1865. Spoils, remains of ancient statues and capitals, which Prince Karl collected, are set into the walls throughout. HIB

36, 37. Berlin-Zehlendorf (Wannsee), Glienicke, Kasino, 1824/25

This well-proportioned building was the first of the Glienicke buildings to be erected by Schinkel, in 1824/1825, and is a conversion of an old billiard house. The plaster articulation emphasizes the horizontals, and there are large bowls on the roof corners. The most striking element is provided by the two pergolas, creating a connection between the building and nature. There is false Pompeian architecture on the side of the casino, which has an exedra bench in front of it. There used to be a small Pompeian garden here. Inside, behind an ante-room, is the small hall or »Middle Salon« with divided fields in marble stucco and a large metal chandelier. The room was completely redesigned by Prince Karl in the 1870s. HIB

38. Berlin-Zehlendorf (Wannsee), Pfaueninsel, Schweizerhaus, 1829/30

Just on the left up the hill behind the mooring point, almost hidden among the trees, is the Schweizerhaus, which Schinkel built in 1829/30 as a gardener's house. It fitted in with a current fashion, a longing for simple, rural things. The Swiss chalet, hidden in a mountain valley, was seen as a primitive type of house or temple, the primeval hut. The scratches on the plinth plaster simulate a cyclopean wall, the door- and window-frames and the cornices are carved in wood and painted with arabesque patterns and palmettes. The open entrance steps run directly into the building, and there are two piers with hints of capitals flush with the house wall. This very modest entrance arrangement is reminiscent of the stairwell of the Altes Museum (ill. 12) as a connection between interior and exterior. The roofs of the gable walls protrude considerably. HIB

39. Berlin-Zehlendorf (Wannsee), Pfaueninsel, Kavalierhaus, 1824–26

A late-Gothic patrician house in Brodbänkengasse in Danzig was pulled down in 1823, and the façade was acquired by the crown prince. Schinkel was commissioned to place this façade in front of a domestic building in the middle of the island that had been erected by Friedrich Ludwig Carl Krüger in 1804. This consisted of a set of rooms between two towers. The Danzig façade was rebuilt in front of the taller south tower, and the façade of the rest of the building was redesigned and adapted in the Gothic style, thus producing a building that was as uniform as it was unusual. HIB

40. Potsdam, Pfingstberg, Pomona-Tempel, 1800 to 1801

Like almost all the other high points around Potsdam, the hill called Pfingstberg since 1817 was used for the cultivation of grapes. A »temple de Pomone« mentioned there was replaced by a new building in 1800. The building completed in 1801 is to be seen as Schinkel's first independent building. Friedrich Wilhelm IV's architectural fantasies seemed to put a question-mark against its existence. But when the project was scaled down, and Lenné's 1862 garden plan carried out, its conspicuous position with wide views over Potsdam was assured. The building was wantonly destroyed in recent decades, but reconstructed from the remnants in 1990. HSCH

41, 42. Potsdam, Alter Markt, Nikolaikirche, 1830–37

Friedrich Gilly designed a new building a year after the parish church in Potsdam burned down in 1795, combining the basic idea of the Pantheon with the autonomy of revolutionary architecture. The shallow dome can scarcely be seen behind the high façade with a Doric portico in front of it. When Schinkel was making new plans in 1826–29 and had to address the king's desire for a twin-towered basilica, the crown prince spoke up for the domed form. Schinkel took over the large Diocletian windows and the portico in the building started in 1830, but opted for the Corinthian order. He implemented the idea of central planning, but changed Gilly's arena-like circle into a Greek cross. Even though the plans were worked out in detail, Persius and Stüler were not able to build the dome with the four corner towers that had been added for statical reasons until 1843. The church was badly damaged in the Second World War, and acquired a new dome in 1953–60; the exterior and its portico were restored by 1975, the interior by 1981. HSCH

43–48. Potsdam, Sanssouci, Schloss Charlottenhof, 1826–29

in 1825 the little farm in the south-western part of the Sanssouci park that has been acquired and developed by Johann Boumann the Elder and also owned for a time by Johann Büring and Carl von Gontard came on the market. Peter Joseph Lenné saw his chance to extend royal gardens. When the Crown acquired the land he put forward a first plan for a new design, and Schinkel was commissioned to redesign the farmhouse. The crown prince, as client, contributed over 100 sketches to the planning process. He called Charlottenhof »my Siam«, seen as synonymous with a better world. Thus he was pursuing his intentions of presenting the way he would rule in future, striving for a harmonious balance of all classes and interests. Charlottenhof is the only work of Schinkel's to have survived completely inside and outside, surrounded by Lenné's landscaped garden, which has been maintained in equally good condition. It has been open to the public as a museum since the Schlösserverwaltung was established in 1927. HSCH

49–53. Potsdam, Sanssouci, Römische Bäder, 1829–39

From 1829, an establishment for the court gardener was set up next to Schloss Charlottenhof. As a deliberate contrast, the strict right angles of the Schloss precinct were complemented by a freely developed »manifold group of architectural objects« with the gardener's house in the »style of Italian country houses« at the centre of it. Around the tower, containing a water reservoir and a bathing cabin, and part of the »villa«, were stables with accommodation for the stable-boy above it, an arcaded hall, whose roof provided a broad view beyond the boundaries of the garden, a tea pavilion in the form of a temple for the crown prince and the Great Arbour, which brought everything together. The fountain niche beyond the arcaded hall was transformed in a second stage into a ancient vestibule followed by an impluvium, the apodyterium, ending in three conches, and a caldarium with a sunken bathing pool below a skylight. The current name »Römische Bäder« which covers the whole complex, is in fact derived only from this last set of features, a playful adaptation of the ideas of Roman house-building acquired from the excavations in Pompeii that were going on at the time. HSCH

p. 16
C. Brand, Karl Friedrich Schinkel, 1832.

Catalogue Ludwig Persius
All texts by Hillert Ibbeken

1, 2. Berlin-Zehlendorf, Park Glienicke, Jägertor, 1842/43
The gate is at the northernmost point of the Glienicke park, only a few hundred metres west of the Moorlake guest house, and opposite the Heilandskirche in Sacrow (ill. 34, 35). The sides are formed by two walls at right angles to each other and curving slightly, each with three piers with trefoils and pinnacles; the walls are battlemented. The west end of the wall surrounds a large erratic block. The two walls do not touch, however, but leave space in the middle for the actual gate. Its corners are set in four slender, octagonal columns topped with high battlements. The masonry is exposed brickwork. The gate leads to the Jägerhof, built by Schinkel in the English Gothic style in 1828. Persius quotes this motif with a shallow Tudor arch over the way through, supporting ribbed vaulting. A Renaissance coat of arms, presumably acquired by Prince Carl at a later date, is built in over the left-hand, east side gate. Un-der the battlements is a frieze of shaped stone, and two coats of arms with eagles adorn the outside of the gate.

3. Berlin-Zehlendorf, Park Glienicke, power and gardener's house, 1838
The power and gardener's house, built across the slope down to the water, is a little north of Schloss Glienicke on the Havel. The building is the first commission for Prince Carl that Persius executed independently. It combines the technical requirements of a pumping station and water reservoir with the aesthetic of parks and gardens ideally. Purely technically, it would have been better to site the tower with the reservoir at the top of the slope, as this would have given higher water pressure, but such a dominant structure would have considerably detracted from the harmony of the park and its buildings. So the five-storey tower with its deep foundations stands at the bottom of the slope, and attached to its left, half concealed, is the actual little building for the steam engine, which until 1952 contained an 18 hp Egells pump. The tower is articulated by a balcony, a series of slit windows, a triple arcade in the belvedere floor and a concluding row of arches in front of the im-pluvium roof. The copper-lined water reservoir, which was filled with rainwater from the top and with water pumped up from below, was between this and the belvedere. The 25 m high tower, a statical masterpiece, has four internal piers, the chimney and all the pipes are inside as well. The gardener's house is on the area at the top, a conversion of a small earlier building. It is a plain cuboid with finely profiled window moulding strips, taking up the series of slit windows in the tower. A pergola, divided into two, leads to the building, split into two because the actual pergola passage does not go through to the entrance itself, but leads to a square entrance pergola with piers and two columns, thus producing rich articulation. The high arch is a key architectural element of the building, in the middle of the slope, and connecting the tower below with the gardener's house at the top. Here Persius is taking up a motif of combined tower and building that Schinkel often used, as for example in his churches in Müncheberg, Petzow or Krummöls (Silesia). Apart from the aesthetic appeal of a construction like this, the necessity often arises, if the subsoil is poor, to compensate for the higher position of a heavy tower with a small footprint in relation to the other building.

4. Berlin-Zehlendorf, Schloss Glienicke, farmyard, 1845
The farmyard is practically directly on the Potsdam–Berlin road, shortly before the entrance to the Schloss when coming from Berlin. The most striking element of the group of buildings is the accommodation for cows and horses with a tower, separated by a high archway. Persius often used the motif of the arch to connect two parts of a building, as for example in the nearby power and gardener's house or the dairy in the Sanssouci park. Schinkel often used it as well. Petzholtz raised the originally squat tower in 1872; it is not known whether Persius designed the ox's head with baldacchino. The group of buildings was not realized until after Persius's death. A small building originally used as a cake-shop stands directly on the road. It has two storeys and an entrance pergola, and is smoothly rendered. Three double round-arched windows on the long side and two on the narrow side articulate the upper storey; the transoms are linked by a finely profiled cornice. The round-arched motif is taken from the roofed chimney.

5. Berlin-Zehlendorf, Schloss Glienicke, south-east wing, 1844
When entering the Schloss grounds from the Berlin–Potsdam road, the first building to be encountered is the south-east corner of the Schloss. Persius raised this part of the building in summer 1844, when the princely family was away on a long trip to Italy. This wing contained the rooms for the ladies-in-waiting and the princely couple's three children. The attic storey above the narrow cornice has the same plaster ashlar finish as the lower storey. The cast zinc lions on the middle piers of the windows were also Persius's work.

6. Berlin-Zehlendorf, Schloss Glienicke, portico, 1840
Persius decorated the new entrance to the Schloss in the east wing with a portico with Doric columns and piers on Attic bases. The roof is adorned, reading from top to bottom, with palmettes all the way round the eaves, below them egg-and-dart moulding, and then a lively frieze with figures of recumbent women, a putto riding on a dolphin and a woman leaning over a kind of sea-cow. This frieze with figures is said to be the work of Schinkel. Underneath this is a leaf-like frieze, and at the very bottom an astragal, a string of pearls, with little discs in between.

7, 8. Berlin-Zehlendorf, Schloss Glienicke, stibadium, 1840
The stibadium is on the south side of Schloss Glienicke and forms the boundary to the garden on the east side by the access road. The exedra, which opens to the west with a view of Potsdam, is covered with a velum, a wooden roof gathered like an awning; the ceiling fields are painted with arabesques and depictions of gods. The semicircular roof is supported on eight small Doric columns on the rear wall; a cast zinc caryatid by Kiss used to stand in the centre of the radial roof, and was replaced by this marble figure at a later date. It is possible that this stibadium is also a Roman quotation, as Pliny the Elder reports that in his country seat there was a stibadium with water flowing out of pipes underneath it, and opposite was a spring. This situation also applies to Glienicke, where a spring flows out from under the stibadium through a lion's head. The sightline from the stibadium to the west is important, looking towards Potsdam, though it is impaired by the present vegetation.

9. Bornim, Max-Eyth-Allee, farm tower, 1844/45
The farm tower is about 1.5 km north of the little town of Bornim near Potsdam, on a low hill a little above the Sacrow-Paretzer-Kanal to the north and the Fahrlander See. The tower and the little wall next to it are the only surviving features, the pitiful remains of an imposing and complex economy farmstead designed and built by Persius in 1844/45, in other words shortly before his death. The farmstead went up in flames when the Red Army invaded in 1945, the remains were removed in 1956 to 1961, only the tower and the little wall have survived. The tower was used in its day to check on the farmhands as they worked in the fields, it now carries a mobile phone mast. It is in yellow brick, shot through with green brick after every fourth layer. The only decoration other than three narrow window slits on each side is a loggia with four openings and round arches and a narrow impost band around the tower. The motif of gaps in the little wall recurs in the parapet walls of the loggia. The tower was originally linked with the farmhouse by a passageway with four arches. The fourth arch, now walled up, survives in the tower base.

10. Bornstedt, Eichenallee / Amundsenstraße, Bornstedter Durchstich, 1843/44
The Bornstedter Durchstich, a ditch, is west of Bornstedt, near the Eichenallee/Amundsenstraße junction. Friedrich Wilhelm IV commissioned Persius to design a bridge in the from of a Roman viaduct. Four high piers carry the round arches, the bridge is built of Rüdersdorf limestone. The original masonry parapet had fallen into disrepair, and was replaced by a wooden railing during refurbishment in 1997–99.

11, 12. Potsdam, Park Babelsberg, power house, 1843/44
The power house is below Schloss Babelsberg immediately by the water on the Glienicker Lake, exactly on the sightline from the pergola at the Schloss to the Schäferberg, where a semaphore station used to stand on the site of the present post-office tower. The power house is a point de vue for everyone coming from the main park entrance. It was commissioned by Prince Wilhelm, who wanted to have fountains at Babelsberg as well. The site foreman was M. Gottgetreu, who was also responsible for later modifications. Stylistically, Persius followed the »Norman« style of Schloss Babelsberg chosen by Schinkel, but used no round-arched windows and armed the whole building with battlements. A tower with a square ground plan corresponds diagonally opposite on the other corner of the building with the very dominant, round chimney, which concludes in a slender, octagonal tower at the top. The chimney is decorated with a spiral band of green glazed tiles. Several cubic buildings are fitted together asymmetrically and decorated with little bay-window turrets. All the roofs are impluvium roofs. The machine hall was lit with a toplight. Surprisingly, the engine operator's accommodation was part of the hall, and there were also guest rooms on the top floor. The 40 hp steam engine, which forced the water in the fountains by the lake shore up to a height of almost 41 m, was so

quiet that it was possible to use the building in this flexible way. In order to compensate for the irregularities of the hand-painted tiles in the masonry the mortar in the joints was smoothed with a semicircular fluted pointing trowel, to produce the effect of a smooth wall.

13–16. Potsdam, Park Babelsberg, Schloss, 1844 to 1849

The Schloss is in a dominant position on the Babelsberg above the Glienicker Lake. Schinkel built the eastern section of the group of buildings with Persius as site manager for Prince Wilhelm in a first building phase in 1835–37. The second building phase, 1844–49, in which the west complex was constructed, is largely based on designs by Persius. The dominant elements are the high octagon of the ballroom at the east end and the flag tower group to the west. In between are irregular elements shifting backwards and forwards, with balconies and bay windows, lavishly articulated with cornices, windows in the Tudor style, friezes and buttresses. The building is mainly in exposed brick. The ballroom in the great octagon (ill. 15, 16) rises through both lower floors, and above it are servants' rooms, also with a view into the southern park. The octagon, crowned with battlements like all parts of the Schloss, is designed with great sophistication, with various friezes, window shapes and window framing.

17, 18. Potsdam, Am Grünen Gitter 3, Friedenskirche, 1844–48

The Friedenskirche, with the Marlygarten and the pool constructed by Lenné, is on the extreme periphery of the Sanssouci park. Friedrich Wilhelm IV decided that the basilica of San Clemente in Rome should be the model, and the church was also to accommodate a medieval mosaic he had acquired in 1835 from San Cipriano on Murano. The base is in Rüdersdorf limestone and a layer of brick, the actual body of the building has plaster ashlar, with different colours imitating different sandstone types. The shallowly inclined zinc roof is decorated with acroteria. The church has a nave and two aisles, with a main and two side apses reflected in the water. The eaves of the main apse are decorated with palmettes above corbel band. The high tower with six open floors and coupled triple arcades quotes the tower of Santa Maria in Cosmedin in Rome. In front of the church on the Marlygarten side is an atrium, an open hall with Doric columns and Attic bases, with Ionic capitals on the church side, as also to be found in the interior. The atrium opens very picturesequely on to the Marlygarten with a double row of arches. The interior, very well lit from clerestory windows, shows the open timber structure of the ceiling; the columns with cast zinc Ionic capitals are in dark marble from the Harz. After Persius's death, the church was completed by L. F. Hesse and F. von Arnim, with site supervision by A. Stüler.

19. Potsdam, Am Neuen Garten 10, dairy, 1843/1844

The dairy – Meierei – is at the extreme northern end of the Neuer Garten, directly on the Jungfernsee. The core of the building had been erected in the neo-Gothic style in 1790–92 as a domestic building, designed by C. G. Langhans and realized by A. L. Krüger. Persius raised the building by one storey and added a tower on a square ground plan in the south-west corner. The south-east corner of the building is articulated by three pointed-arched windows. The battlements are decorated with terracotta stones, with a bracket frieze below them. The dairy business was closed down in 1862 and a power house built, hence the chimney. The building has been used as a brewery-restaurant since 2003.

20. Potsdam, Breite Straße 28, »Mosque«, steam-power plant for Sanssouci, 1841–43

The Sanssouci steam-power plant, the so-called »mosque«, is immediately on the Neustadt Havel bay. This is without doubt Persius's most unusual and highly personal building. That the style should be »in the manner of a Turkish mosque« came from Friedrich Wilhelm IV, and the Borsig engineering works provided the technical equipment, assisted by A. Brix as mechanic and M. Gottgetreu as building supervisor. The aim of the building project was to provide a high performance pumping engine for the Sanssouci water shows, in a picturesque building, because all concerned were rightly afraid that a functional building would ruin the area. Ultimately the architectural style prescribed was that of Cairo rather than Turkey, and the interior is taken over from the mosque in Cordoba and the Alhambra. The exterior appeals because of the clear geometrical forms of cubes placed close to each other, topped by a steep dome above an octagonal substructure and a drum with round-arched windows. Immediately adjacent, in the form of a minaret, is the chimney. The horizontal quality of the building is emphasized by rows of brick glazed in many colours. An octagonal central section with large zigzag bands rises above the parapet of the lower section of the minaret. The tip of the minaret is made up of cast-iron arcades looking as if they have been chased, and a half moon. Inside is the 80 hp steam engine and the pumping mechanism, a bewilderingly complex array of rods, levers and wheels, fitted into the pier structures with trefoil arches and lavish capitals, all in cast iron and painted in many colours, lit by the many windows in the dome. Water is still pumped from here, though with discreet, modern electric pumps, to the mound with ruins north of Schloss Sanssouci, to feed the fountains in the park from there. This is a show that was denied to Frederick the Great because the technology of the day did not permit it.

21. Potsdam, Park Sanssouci, castellan's house, 1840/41

The castellan's house concludes the Sanssouci Schloss complex on the east side. The lower storey, leaning on the slope, was built in 1788 in the manner of a rocky grotto. Friedrich Wilhelm IV wanted it to be raised, to provide accommodation for the court servants. Persius retained the axial articulation of the plinth and added structures at the north and south ends, slightly protruding sections with three linked arched windows. The central axis of the building is emphasized by an aedicula by F. von Arnim, which was not added until 1847. There is a bracket frieze under the slightly protruding, relatively flat roof. The building at the south end served as a billiard room, with a view of the picture gallery dome.

22. Potsdam, Leipziger Straße 7/8, quartermaster's stores with granary, 1844/45

The quartermaster's stores and granary are on Leipziger Straße between the Brauhausberg and the Havel. The large Baroque predecessor building had a hip roof; it did not satisfy Friedrich Wilhelm IV as a point de vue that had a considerable impact on the landscape when seen from the water and the Lustgarten. He commissioned Persius to beautify the façade. Round-arched and rectangular windows alternate in the four-storey building; the attic storey for the whole complex is battlemented. A tall tower in the »Norman« style with four bay windows at the corners rises above the building. The building is empty, and falling into disrepair.

23–25. Potsdam, Park Sanssouci, Fasanerie, 1842 to 1844

The Fasanerie is on the south edge of the Sanssouci park between Wildpark station and Schloss Charlottenburg. As the court hunting grounds had been shifted to the game park, Friedrich Wilhelm IV wanted to set up forestry lodges there, the so-called Etablissements, and a Fasanerie (Pheasantry), which latter was intended to form a link with the Sanssouci park, and Schloss Charlottenhof, with its gardens designed by Lenné. Persius was able to develop the Italian villa style with tower and artfully arranged cubes fully for the Fasanerie, without having to take over elements from earlier buildings. The perfect horizontal and vertical articulation of the group of buildings makes an impact on all sides. It was intended both functionally, for pheasant rearing, and also to provide accommodation for two employees and their families. The south loggia with two fauns on the grille was set up as a place where the king could take tea. The Fasanerie is now a dwelling.

26, 27. Potsdam, Park Sanssouci, Hofgärtnerhaus, 1829–32

The Hofgärtnerhaus is part of the Römische Bäder group of buildings, between Charlottenhof and the Handtmann dairy in the south-east of the Sanssouci park. Persius was closely linked as building officer with this building designed and realized by Schinkel. This is, as it were, the parent cell of the Italian villa in the Potsdam architectural landscape: a loose complex of buildings with a variety of juxtaposed cubes, relatively flat, widely protruding roofs, windows in the round-arched style and a tower. Persius took over this building type created by Schinkel and designed it following the numerous variants available from his Potsdam villas. The building is now used as a dwelling and for exhibitions.

28. Potsdam, Park Sanssouci, Ruinenberg, Normannischer Turm, 1845/46

The Normannischer Turm stands on the Ruinenberg on Schloss Sanssouci's northern sightline. A set-piece ruin was already here, consisting of a wall fragment from a Roman circus, a circular Doric temple and three Ionic columns, reflected in a large pool, the reservoir for the park's water features. The king wanted a lookout tower here, so that he would be able to survey the landscape park designed by Lenné, and there was also to be a tearoom. Persius submitted a design that the king approved, and the tower was completed in Rüdersdorf quarry limestone by F. von Arnim after Persius's death. The tower leans directly on the circus wall and is decorated with battlements.

29. Potsdam, Park Sanssouci, Ruinenberg, exedra, 1843/44

The exedra is on the west flank of the Ruinenberg opposite the Bornstedt crown estate. The semicircular bench with gryphon's feet as armrests is derived from the bench by the grave of the priestess Mamia in the Street of Tombs in Pompeii, which Goethe sat on during his visit to Campagna in 1787. Friedrich Wilhelm IV had benches of this kind places in many striking landscape positions. The photograph is an attempt to recreate a water-colour by Carl Graeb.

30, 31. Potsdam, Park Sanssouci, Schloss Sanssouci, annexes, 1840–42

These annexes are adjacent to Schloss Sanssouci to the east and west. They became necessary because the earlier buildings did not provide sufficient space for Friedrich Wilhelm IV's expanded court. The long buildings, extended by several axes, are so skilfully matched to the north façade of the Schloss with its Corinthian pilasters that they hardly look like new additions. The fronts have porches with three arches. The east extension accommodates the kitchen, the bakery and the wine cellar, the upper rooms are used by the kitchen staff. The kitchen with its original oven, cast-iron columns and roof supports is Persius's design, realized by F. von Arnim. The ladies-in-waiting and male courtiers lived in the west extension, the ladies' wing. Access to the rooms was by staircases at the ends of the building, there are no corridors, but an enfilade on both storeys. The design of the Traumzimmer (Dream Room) arose from a dream by Friedrich Wilhelm IV, the Tapetenzimmer (Wallpaper Room) on the top floor has a skylight. The ladies' wing was the first to have water-closets.

32. Potsdam, Maulbeerallee, stibadium in the Paradiesgärtlein, 1841–48

The stibadium is a little to the west below the Orangerieschloss on Maulbeerallee in the botanical garden. The stibadium or atrium, a place of contemplation, is a square structure, open at the top, with an impluvium roof, just as in Schinkel's Römische Bäder. An extension on the west side ends in a semicircular apse, there are portals to the north and south and an aedicula on the east side. The entablature at the top, a triglyph metope frieze, does not support a roof, but sits on the narrow internal roof cornice. The square of the central pool is surrounded by a row of terra-cotta columns with Corinthian capitals. The pool contains a sculpture by F. L. Bürde (1846) featuring a large eagle striking a stag. The room on the west side has a heavy coffered ceiling, the apse is decorated with Pompeian motifs: herms, birds and garlands. The stibadium was designed in close co-operation with the king.

33. Potsdam, Am Grünen Gitter 5/6, Villa Illaire, 1843–46

The Villa Illaire is at the east end of the Sanssouci park. The earlier single-storey building from the 18th century was occupied by the court gardener Sello, and then by his successor Voss. At the king's request, Persius designed a conversion for Kabinettsrat Illaire. This produced a richly articulated group of buildings with flat impluvium roofs of different heights. Only the base storey has plaster ashlar, the upper floor, smoothly rendered, is articulated by sharply incised rectangular windows with cast zinc figures on the upper windows. Only on the street façade is there a large, round-arched window over the balcony, a window of the kind found in Roman baths, with sturdy putti as caryatids. A pergola creates a link with the apprentices' house at the front on the west side. The relatively austere north aspect, on the Schloss side, is decorated by an aedicula window added at the ex-

press wish of Friedrich Wilhelm IV. The individual sections of the central building are connected by a striking bracket frieze immediately below the eaves. A pool was placed in the Marlygarten, which is adjacent on the east side.

34, 35. Sacrow, Krampitzer Straße, Heilandskirche, 1843/44

The Sacrow church, still under the jurisdiction of Potsdam, is directly on the banks of the Havel as it flows down from the Pfaueninsel and broadens out into the Jungfernsee. This church is perhaps Persius's most famous building. It is based on a schematic sketch by Friedrich Wilhelm IV, who also chose the site. The king often visited the building, and laid down a number of details. From the outside, and particularly from the opposite bank, the building looks like a basilica with a nave and two aisles. The impression is given by the round-arched arcade hall that surrounds the church completely. The columns are in sandstone, the capitals in cast zinc. Above the arcades is a powerful bracket frieze with palmettes. The whole building is clad in brick, shot through with layers of blue-glazed tiles with rosettes, emphasizing the church's horizontal quality. Five conspicuous clerestory windows with round arches provide the church with light; apart from the entrance, the west gable side has only a rose window. A large, rectangular forecourt is bordered on the north side by the free-standing campanile, and on the south side by a round bench with a tall cross. The church's plain interior is defined by the open roof truss with wooden beams and the windows, placed at a great height, with carved wooden figures of the Apostles by J. Alberty between them. The paintwork in the apse is by C. Begas. The organ around the rose window is a dummy. The church, which stands right in the former GDR border area, was under considerable threat for a time, but it was possible to restore it completely.

p. 62
F. Jentzen, Ludwig Persius, ca. 1843.

Catalogue Friedrich August Stüler
The catalogue texts are abridged versions of texts from: Eva Börsch-Supan and Dietrich Müller-Stüler, *Friedrich August Stüler, 1800–1865*, Deutscher Kunstverlag, Munich and Berlin, 1997, with additional observations by Hillert Ibbeken.

1, 2. Berlin-Charlottenburg, Spandauer Damm / Schloßstraße junction, former Garde-du-Corps-Kasernen, 1851–59

The king asked for two barracks to be built opposite Schloss Charlottenburg in 1844. Building was delayed un-til 1844 because of complications over purchasing the plot. Work finished in 1859. The clearly articulated cube is the same when viewed from all sides. The building has seven axes, the middle three axes project slightly and are topped with gables that interrupt the balustrade running round the building. The base of the three-storey building is in ashlar, the two upper storeys are smoothly rendered and articulated with pilasters ending in Corinthian capitals with eagles and spread wings. The building is topped by a bracket cornice and a band of circular windows. The dominant element is a central dome on the roof intended to relate to the Schloss and presumably not to Stüler's design. Sixteen columns with terracotta capitals supplied by March support a frieze with leaf decoration and helmets, and above this is the ribbed hemisphere of the dome. The building was damaged in the war and restored in the 1950s, and now houses the Berggruen Museum. The illustrations show the west building; the two are identical.

3–5. Berlin-Marzahn, Alt Marzahn, Prot. village church, 1870/71

The church was designed as early as 1857, replacing a 13th-century rubblestone church, which was pulled down; it was one of over fifty old village churches in Berlin. The yellow brick building is well preserved and cared for. It is very small, with five axes, and striking buttresses defining the exterior. On the choir side is a high stepped gable, and the tower gables under a simple double arch are also stepped. A simple decorative band of crosses in moulded brick is placed under the eaves cornice. The small rectangular choir is pushed up against the body of the building. The interior surprises with a wide ribbed vault and a carefully restored horseshoe gallery on small supports forms six arches. The church is in excellent condition, but the original decoration was destroyed when the building was restored in 1962 and 1982/83.

6, 7. Berlin-Mitte, Bodestraße 3, Alte Nationalgalerie, 1867–76

The building was realized by Johann Heinrich Strack in 1867–76, in other words after Stüler died. Stüler had designed the building in 1862–65, taking sketches by Friedrich Wilhelm IV into account. The idea for the building is based on a design by Friedrich Gilly for a monument to Frederick the Great, who had so caught the imagination of the then sixteen-year-old Schinkel in 1797. The temple-like structure on a 12 m high base in the form of a Roman pseudodipteros was intended to make an impact on the cityscape from a distance, and succeeded. The main façade is defined by free-standing Corinthian columns, and the other façades have Corinthian half-columns with the names of German artists chiselled between them. The windows are not very conspicuous. This is the first quarrystone building in Berlin, after the Brandenburg Gate. Moritz Schulz's relief on the main gable shows Germania as the protectress of the arts, and above this is Rudolf Schweinitz's group of the three fines arts, on top of the gable. There is a large double flight of steps in front of the building, and the round-arched entrance is on the ground floor, between its side pieces. Above this is the equestrian statue of Friedrich Wilhelm IV, a work in bronze by Alexander Calandrelli, 1882. The rear façade has an exedra running across the full height of the Nationalgalerie. It is topped by a richly mobile, undulating pictorial frieze and a bracket cornice above a palmette frieze. The building was badly damaged in the war and rebuilt as early as the 1950s, and a second restoration phase lasted until 2001. Nothing has survived of Stüler's interior architecture. The building is in very good condition.

8, 9. Berlin-Mitte, Bodestraße 4, Neues Museum, 1843–46, 1855, 1865

The illustrations from the Neues Museum show its ruinous condition in May 2003, giving only an inkling of it former splendour. The neoclassical building in the Schinkel tradition is Friedrich Wilhelm IV's most important building and Stüler's main work, alongside the National Musem in Stockholm and the Academy in Budapest. It was designed in 1841, built from 1843–46 and not completed until 1855 because of the 1848 revolution, the staircase not being painted until 1865. This building extended the Museum Island, predominantly a harbour in its northern section, into a magnificent museum landscape. This was needed because the collections were growing and there was increasing interest in other art fields. Like the Altes Museum, the Neues Museum is grouped around two inner courtyards. The central section is topped with gables adorned with lavish figures, the side projections support domes, with two-storey rotundas inside. The poor subsoil demanded a light building, but it had to be able to accommodate heavy exhibits. Stüler solved this problem professionally and elegantly with wide iron structures, the first of their kind in a large building in Berlin, and with vaults constructed from hollow pots. The building's ruinous state has one regretful advantage: it is possible to see these structural elements clearly. All the galleries were specifically matched to their exhibits.

10, 11. Berlin-Pankow, Breite Straße, Prot. village church, 1857–59

This church is an extension attached to a medieval church. The old church is used as the choir, the new one has a nave and two aisles, the nave being higher and wider. This use of three as a motif is taken up again at the point of connection with the choir, where two lower, narrower arches stand by the high central one. Inside, a wide arch set back against the east wall of the choir gives the impression of an apse, which in fact does not exist. Font and pulpit have survived, the latter shows the Doctors of the Church, including Luther, Zinzendorf and Calvin. Two high, octagonal towers flanking the choir emphasize the border between the old and the new church. A large porch with two ancillary buildings was placed in from ot the west front in 1908, forming a harmonious conclusion to the building. The church is in excellent condition inside and out.

12, 13. Berlin-Tiergarten, Alt-Moabit 25, Prot. church of St. Johannis, 1851–57

The Johanniskirche is one of the suburban churches built by Schinkel, 1833–35. The congregation asked for a parsonage at an early stage. After a few changes to the design, Stüler built the parsonage and school house in 1851–53, the arcaded hall in 1865 and the tower in 1856/57. The tower was in scaffolding for renovation purposes when the photographs were taken. The arcaded hall has eleven axes, with a large porch in the middle in front of the main entrance. The porch has a head of Christ and two hovering angels on the gable, supported by two Corinthian columns in front of Corinthian pilasters. At the sides are four niches with figures of the Evangelists. The arcaded hall is in good condition.

14, 15. Berlin-Tiergarten, Matthäikirchplatz, Prot. church of St. Matthäus, 1844–46

The church building association, founded in 1843, commissioned the design from Stüler, the king became the patron. The church is a hall with a nave and two aisles, the aisles conclude in smaller apses, and the nave in a higher and larger apse. The sides of the six-axis building have two pairs of small round-arched windows on the ground floor, the upper storey and the gable sides have windows in threes, with the middle one slightly raised. The integral tower on the north side is somewhat narrower than the nave. Under its octagonal spire is an arcaded gallery accompanied by four corner turrets developing from the pilaster strips. The gable fronts are clearly separated from each other by narrow niches carrying the gutters. The exposed brick structure with yellow facing bricks is clearly articulated with horizontal red stripes and a string course under the upper windows, the central apse and the gable are decorated with round windows. The church was badly damaged shortly before the end of the war and its exterior was restored in 1956 to 1960. It is in excellent condition. The interior was destroyed and completely changed, but it has outstanding acoustics and is a popular concert venue. There is an almost identical but somewhat smaller Stüler church in Peitz north of Cottbus. The Matthäuskirche is in very good condition.

16, 17. Berlin-Zehlendorf, Prot. church of Peter und Paul auf Nikolskoe, 1834–37

The first reason for the building of this church was the Tsarina's romantic desire to hear church bells ringing on the Pfaueninsel. The king decided on a design by Stüler, and suggestions by the crown prince were accepted as well. The church is on the relatively steeply sloping bank of the Havel opposite the south-western end of the Pfaueninsel, which required the construction of a high base on the north-east side, as the high transepts also suggest. This base supports a central tower, four-cornered at first, then octagonal, with a lavishly decorated dome. The tower is flanked by two triples arcaded halls containing the church's famous peal of bells. A large, central window rose also features a clock. The pilaster strips on the corners of the transepts extend a little above the roof, in exactly the same way as the church at Christdorf, which is very similar to the Nikolskoe church. The high single room has four round-arched windows and an apse with five round windows. The rear gable is decorated with dark red brick squares, and a cornice runs almost the whole of the way round the church. The great portal, whose archivolt is inlaid with terracotta

bricks with plant motifs, is under the wooden porch in the Russian style. All the church's exposed masonry is executed accurately. The interior has survived equally well with the original decoration and furnishings. The deeply articulated coffered ceiling corresponds with the top sections of the galleries running right round the space. The great triumphal arch in front of the apse finds its counterpart in the equally large arch for the organ niche. The spandrels of the arches contain four painted tondi showing the Evanelists. The capitals of the octagonal, slender gallery pillars are rather like wayside shrines, with pictures of angels and acanthus leaves. One special feature is the high pulpit on four pillars with Corinthian capitals and winged angels' heads. The basket carries oval mosaics of St. Peter and Paul. The court pew was opposite the pulpit at the same level. The church has been outstandingly well looked after.

18, 19. Berlin-Zehlendorf, Wilhelmplatz, Prot. village church, 1858/59

This cruciform church in the round-arched style stands on a hill above the Stöpchensee, in a dominant position. The king commissioned it to Stüler. Like all the other parts of the building, the mighty tower above the crossing carries pilaster strips on its corners, here topped with pinnacles. The choir and transepts are arranged as five-part conches, the single-aisled nave has three axes, and its walls too are articulated with pilaster strips. The yellow, exposed masonry with red horizontal stripes has survived in excellent condition. The west façade has a large rose window following a Romanesque, Italian model. In the interior, the crossing arches develop from the piers without imposts. When the church was restored in the early 1990s the space was painted white overall, instead of lightly applied, sandstone-coloured ashlar painting, thus creating an unfavourable contrast with the ceilings, which are painted in far too dark a colour. The beamed ceiling of the nave is flat, that of the crossing and conches relatively steep. The octagonal pulpit on slender columns shows standing figures of the Apostles. The church contains a magnificent tomb for the Heydert family of court gardeners, dating from 1777. The church is in a good condition.

20, 21. Caputh, Straße der Einheit, Prot. church, 1850–52

Caputh lies somewhat south of Potsdam on the Templiner and Schwielow See. The church is close to the early Baroque princely palace. The king had rejected a rebuilding plan by the Potsdam government and commissioned Stüler to produce a new design and gave advice about details like the tower design. The church is a gallery basilica with nave, two aisles and five bays in the Italian Romanesque style, like San Zeno in Verona, for example. Parts of the walls from the previous building were retained at the king's request. The lavishly articulated south-west façade has decorative ashlar work with yellow brickwork on the pilaster strips and at the corners of the building. The main gable contains a large rose window, the small gable in the porch has five-part round-arched windows, rising to the centre. The tall, free-standing bell tower rises on the north-west side, the street side, and is linked to the nave by a small intermediate corridor with a sacristy. The tower is square at its base and moves into an octagonal section whose corner pilaster strips articulate the building clearly. Above this is a shallow cap with a cross. In the interior the arches are supported by piers with slender corner columns, topped with cushion capitals, the coffered ceiling is flat. The original organ case has survived, and a large triumphal arch with a banderole soars up in front of the apse. The two large chandeliers are connected to each other by ingenious cables and pulleys. The church was excellently restored after the fall of the Berlin Wall, and is in very good condition.

22. Caputh, Marienquelle, 1855
The design for the brickwork housing the spring goes back to a suggestion from the king, who wanted the tomb of Mary in the Kidron valley near Jerusalem to be used as model. The Marienquelle (Spring of Mary) is about 400 m north of the Caputh boundary the side of the embankment road, quite lonely in the dense woodland. In front of it is the spring pool, with no discernible signs of any containing masonry. The structure consists of a plain yellow brick wall with lower continuations at the sides, and three wide pointed arches in red brick staggered one above the other, reminiscent of Saracen forms. The two outer arches are supported by four columns, behind the inner arch with the actual outlet for the spring water is a rendered square with spandrels carrying two tondi with badly damaged reliefs. The spring was renovated some years ago, and a later, disfigurement by graffiti was also removed.

23, 24. Potsdam, Park Sanssouci, Orangerieschloß and Raffaelsaal, 1850–60
Friedrich Wilhelm IV was very taken with the villas in the vicinity of Rome, and even when he was still crown prince he planned to top the hill north-west of Sanssouci with a complex consisting of orangery halls and a palace or villa. Raphael's unfinished Villa Madama was one of the changing Roman models. Persius produced designs with a central section containing a theatre from 1840, and from 1847 the »Palladio motif« (central arch, entablature straight at the sides) appears in the king's sketches as the key design element. In April 1850, after the Pfingstberg design was completed, Stüler came up with the final form for the building in three sketches, each of which the king changed: central section with courtyard in front, two-tower section between colonnades (with an extensive view over Sanssouci), orange galleries given rhythm by wide piers, narrow but deep side buildings. Here Palladian arches open up the 300 m long terrace and the view from the Heilig-Geist-Kirche to the Belvedere – the »direction line« of the planned high road whose glittering conclusion was to be the Orangerie, with Gustav Bläser's 1873 statue of Friedrich Wilhelm IV in the central arch.

25–27. Potsdam, Ribbeckstraße, Prot. church, 1855/1856
A preliminary design by Ludwig Persius existed for this church, as well as several designs by Stüler. A particular problem was caused by its direction towards the cemetery, as the smallest possible number of graves had to be destroyed. This church in the round-arched style is a single room with four axes with yellow facing bricks from Joachimsthal. The corners carry baldacchinos with terracotta Apostle figures. The west side with the entrance in the form of a portal with gable is decorated with a large rose window an and a small bell-cage on the gable. The sides of the nave each have three coupled round-arched windows between the pilaster strips. A choir by Reinhold Persius, the son of Ludwig Persius, was added

in 1881–83. The beamed ceiling inside is flat and very dark, and this also applies to the galleries, which are supported by transverse wooden arches. As there are no windows under the galleries, the church is relatively dark. An arcade of nine round arches with a gable roof concludes the church on the street side, ending in a small single-axis end building on the south side and the large campanile on the north side. The arcade has a parapet with tightly arranged small double columns with small capitals and round arches on the street side. The tower is articulated by slightly protruding corner pilaster strips and a central pilaster strip and has two round-arched windows in each of the five storeys. Its roof is a shallow pyramid over a round-arched cornice. The church was restored in 1977–81 and is in very good condition. It is much visited because of the nearby Bornstedt royal demesne.

28. Potsdam, Schopenhauerstraße, Weinbergstor, 1850/51
Stüler prepared two designs and worked on many sketches by the king, who wanted a triumphal arch like the Arch of the Moneychangers in Rome here at the point where Höhenstraße was intended to branch off from what was then Bornstedter Allee. The scene on the rear of the architrave commemorates the suppressed revolt in Rhineland-Palatinate and in Baden, and at the front only the building date appears, innocuously. The terracotta slabs were made by March and Feilner. They show the four cardinal virtues on the front: on the left strength and justice, on the right moderation and wisdom. Underneath, as recumbent figures, are symbols of telegraphy and the railway, and on the back the arts, appropriately. The inner reveals show the troops departing and returning. The structure is in good condition.

p. 98
A. Menzel, Friedrich August Stüler, 1861/62.

Bibliographie

Adler, Friedrich, »Die Bauschule zu Berlin«, *Zeitschrift für Bauwesen*, Bd. 19, 1869, S. 469–475.

Anderson, Stanford, »Schinkel, Behrens, an elemental tectonic, and a new classicism«, in Susan Peik (Hrsg.), *Karl Friedrich Schinkel. Aspects of his Work / Aspekte seines Werkes*, Stuttgart und London 2001, S. 116 bis 124.

Behrendt, Walter Curt, *Modern Building. Its Nature, Problems, and Forms,* New York 1937.

Börsch-Supan, Eva, *Berliner Baukunst nach Schinkel 1840–1870*, München 1977.

Börsch-Supan, Eva, *Stüler und Friedrich Wilhelm IV.*, in: *Stilstreit und Einheitskunstwerk. Internationales Historismus-Symposium Bad Muskau*, Dresden 1997, S. 98 bis 133.

Börsch-Supan, Eva, und Dietrich Müller-Stüler, *Friedrich August Stüler 1800–1865*, München und Berlin 1997.

Breuer, Robert, «Das Haus Wiegand in Dahlem«, *Innendekoration*, 24. Nov. 1913, S. 430–477.

Conrads, Ulrich, »Der andere Mies«, *Bauwelt*, 59, Heft. 38, 16. September 1968.

Fleetwood Hesketh, Roger und Peter, »Ludwig Persius of Potsdam«, *The Architects' Journal*, Juli 1928, S. 77

Friedrich August Stüler und Potsdam, Ausstellungskatalog, Potsdam 2000.

Hitchcock, Henry-Russell, *Modern Architecture: Romanticism and Reintegration*, New York 1928.

Hitchcock, Henry-Russell, »The Traveler's Notebook: The Romantic Architecture of Potsdam«, *International Studio*, 99 (1931), S. 46–49.

Hitchcock, Henry-Russell, *Architecture: Nineteenth and Twentieth Centuries*, Harmondsworth 1958.

Hitchcock, Henry-Russell, und Philip Johnson, *The International Style: Architecture since 1922*, New York 1932.

Ibbeken, Hillert (Hrsg.), *Ludwig Persius. Das architektonische Werk heute / The architectural work today*, Stuttgart und London 2005.

Ibbeken, Hillert (Hrsg.), *Friedrich August Stüler. Das architektonische Werk heute / The architectural work today*, Stuttgart und London 2006.

Ibbeken, Hillert, und Elke Blauert (Hrsg.), *Karl Friedrich Schinkel. Das architektonische Werk heute / The architectural work today*, Stuttgart und London 2002 (2. Auflage).

Karl Friedrich Schinkel. Architektur Malerei Kunstgewerbe, Ausstellungskatalog, Berlin 1981.

Landau, Sarah Bradford, »Richard Morris Hunt, the Continental Picturesque, and the ›Stick Style‹«, *Journal of the Society of Architectural Historians*, 42, Okt. 1983, S. 272–289.

Loos, Adolf, *Architektur* (1910), in: Adolf Loos, *Sämtliche Schriften in 2 Bänden*, Wien und München 1962, Bd. 1, S. 317 f.

Mebes, Paul, *Um 1800. Architektur und Handwerk im letzten Jahrhundert ihrer traditionellen Entwicklung*, München 1908.

Müller-Stüler, Dietrich, »August Stüler. Preußische Baukunst um die Mitte des 19. Jahrhunderts«, *Kunst im Dritten Reich*, 7 (1943), S. 75–88.

Muthesius, Hermann, *Stilarchitektur und Baukunst*, Berlin 1902.

Peik, Susan (Hrsg.), *Karl Friedrich Schinkel. Aspects of his work / Aspekte seines Werkes*, Stuttgart und London 2001.

Peschken, Goerd, *Karl Friedrich Schinkel. Das Architektonische Lehrbuch*, Berlin 1979 (*Karl Friedrich Schinkel. Lebenswerk*).

Poensgen, Georg, *Die Bauten Friedrich Wilhelms IV. in Potsdam*, Berlin 1930.

Poensgen, Georg. »Ludwig Persius, der Nachfolger und Vollender Schinkels in Potsdam«, in: *Schinkel-Almanach, Ausstellung klassizistischer Baukunst der Schinkelzeit, veranstaltet vom Architekten- und Ingenieur-Verein zu Berlin in der National-Galerie zu Berlin (ehemal. Kronprinzenpalais)*, Berlin 1931.

Posener, Julius (Hrsg.), *Festreden Schinkel zu Ehren*, Berlin 1981.

Scheffler, Karl, *Die Architektur der Großstadt*, Berlin 1913.

Scheffler, Karl, *Deutsche Baumeister*, Leipzig 1939.

Schmid, Josef, *Karl Friedrich Schinkel. Der Vorläufer neuer deutscher Baugesinnung*, Leipzig 1943.

Schönemann, Heinz, »Lenné in Berlin«, in: *Peter Joseph Lenné. Katalog der Zeichnungen*, Tübingen und Berlin 1993 (Edition Axel Menges).

Schumacher, Fritz, »Hans Poelzig und Peter Behrens«, in: *Selbstgespräche, Erinnerungen und Betrachtungen*, Hamburg 1949.

Stahl, Fritz (Pseudonym für Siegfried Lilienthal), *Karl Friedrich Schinkel*, Berlin 1911.

Stamp, Gavin, «At once picturesque and classical: Alexander Thomson's Holmwood«, *Journal of the Society of Architectural Historians*, Bd. 57, 1958, Nr. 1, S. 46–58.

Stüler, Friedrich August, *Über die Wirksamkeit König Friedrich Wilhelms IV. in dem Gebiete der bildenden Künste«*, Berlin 1861.

Stüler, Friedrich August und Johann Heinrich Strack, »Die Eisenbahnanlage von Petersburg nach Pawlowsk«, *Architektonisches Album*, 1/2, 1838, Bl. 1–12.

Westheim, Paul, «Mies van der Rohe: Entwicklung eines Architekten«, *Das Kunstblatt*, 11, Nr. 2 (Februar 1927), S. 55–62.

Westheim, Paul, »Schinkel und die Gegenwart«, *Der Baumeister*, 11, Januar 1913, Beilage, S. B81–B84.

Wullen, Moritz, *Die Deutschen sind im Treppenhaus, Der Fries Otto Geyers in der Alten Nationalgalerie*, Köln 2002.

Bibliography

Adler, Friedrich, »Die Bauschule zu Berlin«, *Zeitschrift für Bauwesen*, vol. 19, 1869, pp. 469–475.

Anderson, Stanford, »Schinkel, Behrens, an elemental tectonic, and a new classicism«, in Susan Peik (ed.), *Karl Friedrich Schinkel. Aspects of his Work / Aspekte seines Werkes*, Stuttgart and London, 2001, pp. 116 to 124.

Behrendt, Walter Curt, *Modern Building. Its Nature, Problems, and Forms,* New York, 1937.

Börsch-Supan, Eva, *Berliner Baukunst nach Schinkel 1840–1870*, Munich, 1977.

Börsch-Supan, Eva, *Stüler und Friedrich Wilhelm IV.*, in: *Stilstreit und Einheitskunstwerk. Internationales Historismus-Symposium Bad Muskau*, Dresden, 1997, pp. 98 to 133.

Börsch-Supan, Eva, and Dietrich Müller-Stüler, *Friedrich August Stüler 1800–1865*, Munich and Berlin, 1997.

Breuer, Robert, «Das Haus Wiegand in Dahlem«, *Innendekoration*, 24 Nov. 1913, pp. 430–477.

Conrads, Ulrich, »Der andere Mies«, *Bauwelt*, 59, no. 38, 16 September 1968.

Fleetwood Hesketh, Roger and Peter, »Ludwig Persius of Potsdam«, *The Architects' Journal*, July 1928, pp. 77

Friedrich August Stüler und Potsdam, exhibition catalogue, Potsdam, 2000.

Hitchcock, Henry-Russell, *Modern Architecture: Romanticism and Reintegration*, New York, 1928.

Hitchcock, Henry-Russell, »The Traveler's Notebook: The Romantic Architecture of Potsdam«, *International Studio*, 99 (1931), pp. 46–49.

Hitchcock, Henry-Russell, *Architecture: Nineteenth and Twentieth Centuries*, Harmondsworth, 1958.

Hitchcock, Henry-Russell, and Philip Johnson, *The International Style: Architecture since 1922*, New York, 1932.

Ibbeken, Hillert (ed.), *Ludwig Persius. Das architektonische Werk heute / The architectural work today*, Stuttgart and London, 2005.

Ibbeken, Hillert (ed.), *Friedrich August Stüler. Das architektonische Werk heute / The architectural work today*, Stuttgart and London, 2006.

Ibbeken, Hillert, and Elke Blauert (eds.), *Karl Friedrich Schinkel. Das architektonische Werk heute / The architectural work today*, Stuttgart and London, 2002 (2nd edition).

Karl Friedrich Schinkel. Architektur Malerei Kunstgewerbe, exhibition catalogue, Berlin, 1981.

Landau, Sarah Bradford, »Richard Morris Hunt, the Continental Picturesque, and the ›Stick Style‹«, *Journal of the Society of Architectural Historians*, 42, Oct. 1983, pp. 272–289.

Loos, Adolf, *Architektur* (1910), in: Adolf Loos, *Sämtliche Schriften in 2 Bänden*, Vienna and Munich, 1962, vol. 1, pp. 317 f.

Mebes, Paul, *Um 1800. Architektur und Handwerk im letzten Jahrhundert ihrer traditionellen Entwicklung*, Munich, 1908.

Müller-Stüler, Dietrich, »August Stüler. Preußische Baukunst um die Mitte des 19. Jahrhunderts«, *Kunst im Dritten Reich*, 7 (1943), pp. 75–88.

Muthesius, Hermann, *Stilarchitektur und Baukunst*, Berlin, 1902. English edition: *Style-Architecture and Building-Art: Transformations of Architecture in the Nineteenth Century and Its Present Condition*, Santa Monica, 1994.

Peik, Susan (ed.), *Karl Friedrich Schinkel. Aspects of his work / Aspekte seines Werkes*, Stuttgart and London, 2001.

Peschken, Goerd, *Karl Friedrich Schinkel. Das Architektonische Lehrbuch*, Berlin, 1979 (*Karl Friedich Schinkel. Lebenswerk*).

Poensgen, Georg, *Die Bauten Friedrich Wilhelms IV. in Potsdam*, Berlin, 1930.

Poensgen, Georg. »Ludwig Persius, der Nachfolger und Vollender Schinkels in Potsdam«, in: *Schinkel-Almanach, Ausstellung klassizistischer Baukunst der Schinkelzeit, veranstaltet vom Architekten- und Ingenieur-Verein zu Berlin in der National-Galerie zu Berlin (ehemal. Kronprinzenpalais)*, Berlin, 1931.

Posener, Julius (ed.), *Festreden Schinkel zu Ehren*, Berlin, 1981.

Scheffler, Karl, *Die Architektur der Großstadt*, Berlin, 1913.

Scheffler, Karl, *Deutsche Baumeister*, Leipzig, 1939.

Schmid, Josef, *Karl Friedrich Schinkel. Der Vorläufer neuer deutscher Baugesinnung*, Leipzig, 1943.

Schönemann, Heinz, »Lenné in Berlin«, in: *Peter Joseph Lenné. Katalog der Zeichnungen*, Tübingen and Berlin, 1993 (Edition Axel Menges).

Schumacher, Fritz, »Hans Poelzig und Peter Behrens«, in: *Selbstgespräche, Erinnerungen und Betrachtungen*, Hamburg, 1949.

Stahl, Fritz (pseudonym for Siegfried Lilienthal), *Karl Friedrich Schinkel*, Berlin, 1911.

Stamp, Gavin, «At once picturesque and classical: Alexander Thomson's Holmwood«, *Journal of the Society of Architectural Historians*, vol. 57, 1958, no. 1, pp. 46–58.

Stüler, Friedrich August, *Über die Wirksamkeit König Friedrich Wilhelms IV. in dem Gebiete der bildenden Künste«*, Berlin, 1861.

Stüler, Friedrich August, *Das Neue Museum zu Berlin*, Berlin, 1862.

Westheim, Paul, «Mies van der Rohe: Entwicklung eines Architekten«, *Das Kunstblatt*, 11, no. 2 (February 1927), pp. 55–62.

Westheim, Paul, »Schinkel und die Gegenwart«, *Der Baumeister*, 11, January 1913, supplement, pp. B81–B84.

Wullen, Moritz, *Die Deutschen sind im Treppenhaus, Der Fries Otto Geyers in der Alten Nationalgalerie*, Cologne, 2002.